TEN
TENERIFE

AMAZING EXPERIENCES

DISCOVERY TOURS

PULL-OUT MAP

Travel with **Insider Tips**

MARCO POLO HIGHLIGHTS

CASAS DE LOS BALCONES ★4
This is where Tenerife's rulers and aristocrats used to hang out. You can still feel their presence in the middle of La Orotava.

➤ p. 51, The Northwest & Teide National Park

BARRANCO DEL INFIERNO ★1
A descent to hell? It might seem like it at first but this is really a piece of paradise with a waterfall.

➤ p. 114, The Southwest

LORO PARQUE ★5
Parrots, penguins, sea lions and whales, all living in recreations of their natural habitat.
📷 *Tip: Sitting in the front row at the orca show will get you a great shot but you (and your camera) will also get very wet!*

➤ p. 45, The Northwest & Teide National Park

GARACHICO ★2
A petite and picturesque town with plenty of colonial history. The huge waves that crash against the coast here are not so quaint.
📷 *Tip: The coastline looks best in the soft light of the setting sun.*

➤ p. 56, The Northwest & Teide National Park

LA LAGUNA ★6
The island's former capital might feel olde worlde but its contemporary bars are the height of cool.
📷 *Tip: The old town is enveloped by shade in the afternoon; visit in the morning for the best photo opportunities.*

➤ p. 77, The Northeast

MASCA ★3
The houses in this ancient village in the rocky Teno Mountains cling to each other for dear life.

➤ p. 61, The Northwest & Teide National Park

SANTA CRUZ DE TENERIFE ★
A successful facelift: world-famous architects have spruced up the capital with creations that include the Palm Gardens on a former rubbish dump and the TEA arts centre.

➤ p. 70, The Northeast

MONTAÑAS DE ANAGA ★
When wispy clouds envelop the evergreen laurels in the Anaga valley, you will feel as if you're in an enchanted forest (photo).

➤ p. 84, The Northeast

WALKING IN THE NATIONAL PARK ★
Huge craters and magnificent rock formations: Parque Nacional del Teide is a geologist's dream.
📷 *Tip: Above 2,000m the air is crisp and clear, so your photos should be ultra-sharp!*

➤ p. 65, The Northwest & Teide National Park

PLAYA DE LAS TERESITAS ★
This beach near Santa Cruz is a real beauty, with a Caribbean flavour. Relax in the shade of the palm trees, and then dive into the turquoise sea, before sipping a cocktail at the beach club.

➤ p. 76, The Northeast

CONTENTS

36 HOLIDAY PLANNER

38 THE NORTHWEST & TEIDE NATIONAL PARK
Puerto de la Cruz & around	42
La Orotava & around	50
Icod de los Vinos & around	54
Garachico & around	56
Parque Nacional del Teide	62

66 THE NORTHEAST
Santa Cruz de Tenerife & around	70
La Laguna & around	77
Tacoronte & around	81
Bajamar, Punta del Hidalgo & around	83
Montañas de Anaga	84

86 THE SOUTHEAST
Candelaria	90
Güímar & around	91
El Médano & around	93
Vilaflor	97

98 THE SOUTHWEST
Los Cristianos & around	102
Playa de las Américas/Costa Adeje & around	107
Los Gigantes & around	116

CONTENTS

MARCO POLO HIGHLIGHTS
2 Top 10 highlights

BEST OF TENERIFE
8 ... green & fair
9 ... on a budget
10 ... with children
11 ... classic experiencees

GET TO KNOW TENERIFE
14 Discover Tenerife
17 At a glance
18 Understand Tenerife
21 True or false?

EATING, SHOPPING, SPORT
26 Eating & drinking
30 Shopping
32 Sport & activities

MARCO POLO REGIONS

36 Holiday planner

DISCOVERY TOURS

124 Tenerife in two days
128 Anaga's laurel forests & an idyllic beach
131 Teno's gorges & gorgeous villages
134 A walk around the Roques de García
136 A cycling tour of the southern uplands

GOOD TO KNOW

140 **HOLIDAY BASICS**
Arrival, Getting around, Emergencies, Essentials, Weather

147 **SPANISH WORDS & PHRASES**
Don't be lost for words

148 **HOLIDAY VIBES**
Books, films, music & blogs

150 **INDEX AND CREDITS**

152 **DOS & DON'TS**
How to avoid slip-ups & blunders

🕐 Plan your visit
€–€€€ Price categories

🍴 Eating/drinking
🛍 Shopping
🍸 Going out
🌴 Top beaches

🌱 Sustainable activities
 Budget activities
 Family activities
🚩 Classic experiences
✓ MARCO POLO Bucket List

(📖 A2) Refers to the removable pull-out map
(0) Located off the map

BEST OF TENERIFE

Trade winds create a blanket of cloud around the peak of Mount Teide

BEST 🍃
GREEN & FAIR

ECO-FRIENDLY ACTIVITIES

THE BEST ISLAND PRODUCE
Tenerife produces excellent wine and goat's cheese, honey from black bees, jam, *mojo* sauces, vinegar and olive oil, all of which are available from market halls *(mercados)* and farmers' markets *(mercadillos del agricultor)*. All purchases support local producers.
➤ p. 30, Shopping

AUTHENTIC SOUVENIRS
Rustic ceramics, unique banana-leaf souvenirs, cigars made from Canarian tobacco: buy these items from the state-owned *Artenerife* stores in order to support the island's craftworkers.
➤ p. 31, Shopping

GET TO KNOW THE ISLAND ONE STEP AT A TIME
Walking is the best way to really get to know Tenerife, its gorges, mountains, wild coasts and deserted bays. Professional walking guides offer their services in all the main holiday resorts. *Hotel Luz del Mar* in Los Silos has a resident guide who leads walks and hiking tours for guests.
➤ p. 35, Sport & activities

ECO-FRIENDLY HOUSES
Photovoltaic, geothermic, wind-powered: find out what these terms mean in practice by visiting the 24 original bioclimatic houses created on Tenerife by *ITER*. Designed by architects from around the world, they prove that we don't have to be reliant on fossil fuels for our energy needs (photo).
➤ p. 96, The Southeast

TAKE THE BUS UP TO 2000M
There are always queues of cars in Teide National Park. If you take the bus instead, not only are you saving money, but you're also doing your bit to protect the landscape. From the south, take *bus 342* to the centre of the island; from the north, it's *bus 348*.
➤ p. 142, Good to know

BEST ON A BUDGET

FOR SMALLER WALLETS

SHIP-SHAPE
The *Casa Museo del Pescador* has more model ships in all shapes and sizes than you could ever imagine.
➤ p. 44, The Northwest & Teide National Park

UNDERSTANDING VOLCANOES
At *El Portillo's* visitor centre you watch geology in real time. The volcanic tube shakes, the lava flows and the room rumbles. Round off your visit with a tour of the botanical rock garden replete with native mountain flora.
➤ p. 64, The Northwest & Teide National Park

THE UNDERGROUND CASTLE
Santa Cruz's main square, the Plaza de España, has a lake and fountains. But the most interesting thing here is underground: the remains of the *Castillo de San Cristóbal* with its massive walls and polished cannons.
➤ p. 73, The Northeast

THE WOW-FACTOR INSIDE & OUT
The wonderful *TEA building* by Herzog & de Meuron is like a walk-in sculpture, and it houses a fantastic, muti-faceted art exhibition – all for free!
➤ p. 74, The Northeast

THE ART OF MEDITATION
The *Fundación Cristino de Vera* in La Laguna combines a beautiful setting with a great collection of art – the perfect atmosphere for reflection and relaxation.
➤ p. 78, The Northeast

SWIMMING ABOVE THE SWELL
It costs nothing to pootle around in *Bajamar's natural swimming pools* while the cliffs around you are battered by huge plumes of spray (photo).
➤ p. 83, The Northeast

BEST WITH CHILDREN

FUN FOR YOUNG & OLD

CLIMBING FUN
Play at being Tarzan at *Forestal Park*. They have ziplines up to 200m long. But don't worry – it is all very safe.
➤ p. 32, Sport & activities

POOLS UPON POOLS
Lago Martiánez is the huge waterpark in Puerto de la Cruz. There are pools, waterfalls, fountains and caves to explore, and palm trees for shade.
➤ p. 45, The Northwest & Teide National Park

ALL CREATURES GREAT & SMALL
Tickets to *Loro Parque* (photo) may be pricey but it will keep the kids happy. There are monkeys, gorillas, meerkats and flamingos as well as daily dolphin, parrot, sea lion and orca shows, and an aquarium stuffed full of tropical fish. Getting there is fun too – take the tourist train from the Plaza Reyes Católicos.
➤ p. 45, The Northwest & Teide National Park

CAMEL RIDES
You have probably always wanted a camel-driving licence – you just weren't aware of it until now. You'll get one at the *Camello Center* if you don a Bedouin costume and take a bumpy ride.
➤ p. 59, The Northwest & Teide National Park

SLIDE THROUGH THE SHARK TANK
The water slides at *Siam Park* are for proper thrill seekers – one even passes through the shark tank! There is also a lazy river and a surfing area as well as a pristine white beach (imported from Portugal) and plenty of wildlife dozing in the sun.
➤ p. 110, The Southwest

BEST 🚩
CLASSIC EXPERIENCES

ONLY ON TENERIFE

A DRAGON?
No-one knows exactly how the *dragon tree (drago)* – actually a lily that can live for 1,000 years – got its name, but its lush crown has become a symbol of Tenerife. The most beautiful specimen is in Icod de los Vinos.
➤ p. 54, The Northwest & Teide National Park

GAZE INTO INFINITY
The *Observatorio del Teide* (photo) is the island's super-modern observatory. Tenerife's consistently clear skies make for great stargazing.
➤ p. 65, The Northwest & Teide National Park

MONUMENTAL PYRAMIDS
The pyramids at *Güímar* suggest that the Canaries were used as a stopping point between the Old and New Worlds long before Columbus, although that theory is disputed …
➤ p. 91, The Southeast

PINE TREES THAT MILK THE CLOUDS
The exceptionally long needles on the Canarian pine means it can "milk" moisture from the clouds while its thick bark protects it from forest fires. One particularly fine example is the *Pino Gordo* in Vilaflor.
➤ p. 97, The Southeast

EAT LIKE A GUANCHE
Gofio, a finely ground roasted grain, was the ultimate staple of the Guanche (early island settlers). For a long time it was derided as "poor people's food" but is now making a comeback as an element of modern Canarian cuisine. You can even get *gofio* mousse at cafés like *El Gomero* in Playa de las Américas.
➤ p. 108, The Southwest

GET TO KNOW TENERIFE

Water-based fun at Lago Martiánez in Puerto de la Cruz

DISCOVER TENERIFE

Eye-catching architecture: Auditorio de Tenerife in Santa Cruz

A mountain full of mystery. Planes circle the Pico del Teide at a respectful distance, before beginning their descent to Tenerife. Visible from miles away, it acts as a signpost and a symbol for the island. Dense cloud cover often separates it from the world below. The king of all volcanoes, it surveys the hostile lunar landscape below from a great height. It's an impressive sight, but for our forebears it was greatly feared. There was an eruption on its northern slopes as recently as 1909.

WRATH OF A GOD

Ancient legends reported the existence of an island called Nivaria, or "snowy place". The Guanche, Tenerife's first settlers, feared that an angry god, Guayote, was orchestrating Teide's eruptions, and Columbus saw the sparks and smoke as

5th century BCE
Settlement by North African Berbers

1496
Alonso Fernández de Lugo conquers Tenerife

16th century
The Canary Islands become Spain's first colony

1706
A volcanic eruption largely destroys the town of Garachico

1852
The Canary Islands become a free trade zone and, as a result, British influence grows

Late 19th century
The cultivation and export of bananas brings economic prosperity to Tenerife

GET TO KNOW TENERIFE

a bad omen for his voyage of discovery. In 1799, Alexander von Humboldt was struck by the fact that at daybreak the first rays of sunshine illuminated the summit, while on the coast darkness still reigned: the Canarian day begins and ends on Pico del Teide (3,718m), Spain's highest mountain.

A BIT OF EVERYTHING

At 2,034km² Tenerife is the largest of the seven "Islands of Eternal Spring", as the Canaries were known to the ancient Greeks. Its diversity is what makes Tenerife so fascinating: blue ocean, great beaches, rugged cliffs and gorges, dense forests, barren wastelands and Pico del Teide rising out of a bizarre sea of rock. Culturally it has a lot to offer too in its colonial towns, museums and galleries. You can sit with the locals in down-to-earth bars, enjoy traditional food, drink their strong wines and share in lively festivals. Surf, dive, hike, cycle, turn night into day or simply lie back and relax — there is no place for boredom on Tenerife. And the sun shines throughout the year.

ELYSIAN WINDS

Arriving at Reina Sofía airport can be something of a shock: barren urban sprawl as far as the eye can see and a parched landscape – water is a rare and precious commodity here. But don't worry, only the southeast is quite this inhospitable. No surprise then that Tenerife's residents have always preferred La Laguna's plateau and the Valle de La Orotava – the island's greenest spot. Northeastern trade winds are responsible for the conditions here, bringing moist air to the north at

1936-39 The Spanish Civil War – which began on the Canary Islands – ushers in Franco's dictatorship

From 1960 Charter flights bring tourists to the islands in large numbers

1975 After Franco's death, Spain becomes a democracy

1986 Spain joins the EU and NATO

2023 Tenerife records its highest-ever visitor numbers: around 6 million!

2024 Many residents protest against the ever-growing number of tourists

altitudes of 700–1,700m. This air collects in the island's mountainous centre and forms clouds which provide rain and much-needed shade, making the area cooler and greener. If you are worried about Saharan temperatures (the west coast of Africa is only 300km away, after all), you will be pleasantly surprised. The climate here is more like a permanent spring – it never gets much hotter than 30°C in summer or cooler than 20°C degrees in winter.

GET INVOLVED IN TENERIFE LIFE!

If you want to get to know the island and its people, you need to explore the Zona Metropolitana, which includes both the old and new capitals. Almost one-third of the 800,000 *Tinerfeños* live in the La Laguna and Santa Cruz area. In recent years the historic centre of La Laguna has been restored and is now free of traffic and has UNESCO World Heritage Site status. In Santa Cruz, internationally renowned architects have designed grand new buildings, such as the Auditorio de Tenerife, the Congress Hall and the TEA arts centre. Ambitious plans for the future include a facelift for the seafront as far as the beach in San Andrés, 10km away, although most of these projects have fallen victim to the global financial crisis.

YES TO TOURISM – BUT NOT TOO MUCH

For many years, the Canary Islands' tourist industry benefitted from instability in other countries, drawing in visitors who would otherwise have holidayed in North Africa or the Middle East. Thanks to the flow of money from the European Central Bank, the Europe-wide financial crisis from 2008 onwards had little effect here. And, even though the Coronavirus pandemic was a huge shock to the system, afterwards Europeans returned to foreign travel like never before, with Tenerife creaming off the majority of visitors to the Canary Islands. But what has been good news for some is bad news for others. Thousands of residential apartments have been converted into lucrative holiday flats, causing rents on the island to rise by over 20% in just one year! For many otherwise tolerant islanders, the situation has become untenable. Slogans, such as "Tourists not welcome!" and "Digital nomads go home!", have begun to appear on the sides of buildings. However, you're unlikely to notice any bad feeling in your daily dealings with the islanders, who remain good-humoured despite their difficulties.

GET TO KNOW TENERIFE

AT A GLANCE

925,000
Inhabitants on the island

Birmingham: 1,158,000

350km
Coastline

Welsh coastline: 1,400km

2,034km²
Surface area

Isle of Wight: 381km²

HIGHEST MOUNTAIN: TEIDE

3,718m
Peak only accessible with a permit

SNOW IS POSSIBLE ON TENERIFE ABOVE 1,500m

AVERAGE LIFE EXPECTANCY:

82.7 years

In the UK: 82.06 years

THE AFRICAN CONTINENT IS 288km AWAY

The Spanish mainland is 1,274km away

SANTA CRUZ

Largest city with 204,000 inhabitants (360,000 incl. La Laguna)
Sunderland has 274,200 inhabitants

"CLOUD-MILKING"
500 litres of water per day are collected from fog

420 LITRES OF WATER are needed to harvest 1kg of bananas

UNDERSTAND TENERIFE

DRAGONS & RED, RED FLOWERS

No plant has captured the imagination of the Canary islanders quite like the dragon tree, which became extinct except on the Macaronesian islands (Canaries, Madeira, Azores, Cape Verde) 20 million years ago, although close relatives do exist in Africa and Asia. The Guanches regarded the tree as sacred, largely because of its resin, known as "dragon's blood", which turns dark red when exposed to the air and which was once used in the preparation of medicinal treatments. If you cut a branch from the *drago*, it grows back as quickly as "the head of a dragon". That is why early naturalists gave the tree its fairytale-inspired botanical name *Dracaena drago*. The locals still revere their dragon trees – there's hardly a garden in the Canary Islands without one.

The Tenerife bugloss *(Echium wildpretii)* is another wonderful plant. Its botanical name refers to the Swiss botanist Hermann Wildpret, but it's a true *Tinerfeño*. It has a 2m-high flower head that grows upwards like a viper

Dragon trees grow up to 20m tall

GET TO KNOW TENERIFE

enchanted by a snake charmer and is studded with thousands of small, glowing red flowers – no bee (or person) can miss it when it is in flower from May to June. The Tenerife bugloss (also known as the "tower of jewels") is hardy and grows well above the treeline – a bright exclamation mark in a volcanic landscape. Close relatives of the Tenerife bugloss grow at lower elevations, but they are smaller and their blossoms are blue or white.

MYSTERIOUS GUANCHES

Little is known about the island's original inhabitants, whose name roughly means "sons of Tenerife". The Guanches colonised the archipelago from the fifth century BCE, arriving in several waves, and it is thought they were descended from the Berbers of North Africa. They were primarily farmers who reared goats and sheep and were ruled by a *mencey* (type of king). When the Spanish settlers arrived on the Canaries, the nine sons of the Mencey Bezenuria were in power. Larger-than-life bronze statues of them line the waterfront promenade of Plaza Patrona de Canarias in Candelaria (see p. 91). The Guanches mostly lived in caves, where they buried their mummified dead.

After Europeans subjugated the native people, the surviving Guanches were quickly integrated into the population of the conquerors. Their legacy can be seen in the *Museo de la la Naturaleza y el Hombre* in Santa Cruz, in *the Museo Arqueológico* in Puerto de la Cruz, and also at the mysterious *Pirámides de Güímar*.

SOS H_2O

The downside of a place where the sun always shines is a shortage of water. Once upon a time there were many rivers on Tenerife and the dense pine and laurel forests absorbed the moisture from the trade winds. Wells and shafts stretching for kilometres, known as galleries, were driven deep into the mountains, reaching underground water supplies, which kept the farmers' crops irrigated. But since then, most of the trees have been felled and many of the wells have run dry. Rainwater is collected in a few reservoirs but it is mainly seawater desalination plants that supply the holiday resorts of Tenerife, whose nine golf courses need huge quantities of water.

The desalination process requires money and energy, which is being generated mainly through the environmentally harmful burning of oil. Newer systems are being developed using a more environmentally friendly osmosis procedure, whereby the salt is mechanically removed from the seawater. The water is forced through a semi-permeable membrane, which lets through the water molecules, but blocks the larger salt particles. Agriculture uses about 70 per cent of the water, while tourism uses about 10 per cent. Please set a good example and don't waste water.

THE MUSIC OF FORTUNE

Barrios Orquestrados is a project that has made its way to the Canary Islands from Venezuela. Children and teenagers from troubled areas, far removed from grand concert halls and conservatoires, learn from professional musicians and have weekly choir sessions with their parents. The idea is to show that creativity and opportunity can help keep young people away from violence.

COLOURFUL CARNIVALS

Months of preparation are needed for Tenerife's exuberant ★ *Carnaval* (carnavaltenerife.com) and the wild weeks in February and March. *Carrozas* or floats have to be built and decorated, costumes sewn and masks carefully crafted. *Murgas* or troupes of jesters, compete with one another to make the best outfits, to sing the cheekiest songs and to play the weirdest music. During the *desfiles* (processions) they dance and frolic noisily through the streets. In Santa Cruz de Tenerife huge seas of wildly celebrating bodies pack every corner of the city.

Each night after these parades, which are transmitted live on national Spanish television, there is a *mogollón*, when *Tinerfeños* dance to Latin beats until the early hours of the morning. And it goes on for days and weeks.

The official climax is the election of the *Reina del Carnaval*. It is not beauty that determines who is crowned carnival queen, but the grace with which she manages to carry the extremely heavy and extravagant costume — itself worth as much as a mid-range car.

No outfit is too flamboyant for a Canarian Carnival

GET TO KNOW TENERIFE

The grand finale of *Carnaval* is the *Entierro de la Sardina*, the burial of the sardine. Once again there is a spectacular, colourful parade, but this time a huge cardboard sardine is dragged through the streets. It ends with a pyrotechnic explosion of Roman candles, rockets and firecrackers. Santa Cruz's *Casa del Carnaval* allows you to soak up the carnival vibes all year round (see p. 71).

INSIDER TIP Missed the carnival? Never mind!

SHADY HOUSES

You may be surprised to see that many elaborately crafted wooden doors and windows are locked up and shuttered and that not a soul can be seen on the splendidly carved balconies. Where the sun beats down all year round, people are more likely to seek shelter in the shade. Closely latticed shutters allow the air to circulate, but they also block the sun, creating an air-conditioning effect.

The façades are gleaming white to reflect the sunlight while exposed stone, door and window frames cut from blocks of rough volcanic stone and pale red roof tiles provide strong contrasts. The hub of a house is the patio, the inner courtyard, which provides access to all the rooms through arcades on each floor. They will often have beautiful plants and there might even be a fountain to create a cool, green retreat from the heat.

Churches and town houses have carved and brightly painted timber ceilings inside – often in the Moorish-inspired Mudéjar style. La Orotava and La Laguna showcase lovely examples of Canarian architecture. The best-preserved mountain village in Tenerife is Masca, where the houses have drystone walls – that is, they use no mortar.

TRUE OR FALSE?

365 DAYS OF SUN A YEAR?

False! There is a very good chance of seeing a sign on the way to Teide directing you to a diversion because the road is *Cortada por nieve* (closed due to snow). It snows across the island at altitudes above 2,000m and the whole of the north is often enveloped in cloud. However, the south does get more than 300 days of sun a year.

VOLCANOES ARE DANGEROUS?

True! The last eruption on Tenerife was in 1909 and geologists think another is due but have no idea if it will be in 1,000, 100 or 2 years. Every spasm on the volcanoes is measured to check if evacuation is needed. The volcano on La Palma, Tenerife's sister island, was kind enough to announce its eruption with a series of quakes in 2021/22.

MADONNA OF THE SEA

A lot of fuss over one tiny statue. A town is named after her, huge events are organised in her honour and taxi drivers display pictures of her in their

Take the cable car up to the wintery world of Teide National Park

cars. The *Virgen de Candelaria* is the crowned queen of Tenerife and has been the island's patron saint for over 500 years. Her career began in the early 15th century when a few Guanches found a Gothic statue of the Madonna and Child, which had been washed ashore near Candelaria. Legend has it that the fearful shepherds wanted to throw stones at it, but their arms became paralysed mid-lob. Impressed by the figure's apparent magical powers, the indigenous Canarians transported the figure into a cave and began to worship it.

When Catholic missionaries arrived on the island, it was easy for them to use this belief to convert the Guanches to the faith of that "magical woman". The statue was given the name Our Lady of Candelaria and a small church was built there in her honour. However, in 1826, a freak wave washed the church and the Madonna out to sea. Today's statue was made in 1827 by a local artist and, of course, a new church was built soon after.

EQUATORIAL ICE
It's only 300km to the Sahara Desert – so can it really snow here? It can, and it does. Teide National Park lies at an elevation of over 2,000m – with the

GET TO KNOW TENERIFE

PUTTING THE CANARY INTO THE CANARY ISLANDS

Its plumage is yellow, its song melodic. Many people are familiar with the canary, but they may not know that it is also the name of an archipelago in the Atlantic.

The domestic canary is a relative of the wild *Serenus canaria*, a bird which still inhabits the forests of the archipelago. It also sings beautifully, but its appearance is not so spectacular, which is why the canary we know today was selectively bred until it acquired its current form.

DON'T GET HURT!

Lucha canaria, Canarian wrestling, dates from the time of the Guanches. Twelve contestants in two teams compete in pairs against each other in a sand-lined ring about 15m in diameter. In a clearly defined starting position they lean forward face-to-face and attempt to grab the rolled-up trouser leg of the opponent with their left hand. During the match, which lasts a maximum of three minutes, the *luchadores* must try, using different grips, to throw their opponent to the ground. If you floor your opponent twice, you win. The team with the most victories wins the contest. If you would like to watch a match, enquire at the tourist information office about fixtures; every major town has its own arena *(terrero de lucha canaria)*.

mountain itself reaching 3,718m – and temperatures can dip below freezing there. When it does snow, Canary Islanders will make the trek to the top in order to enjoy the white stuff.

Snow and ice played an important commercial role on Tenerife at the time of the Spanish conquest. A new occupation, that of ice vendors or *neveros*, emerged. They earned a living from first making the dangerous multi-day ascent to the top of Teide, then transporting their cold cargo, either on donkeys or on their own backs, down into the villages and selling it.

EATING & DRINKING

Gofio, mojo and *bienmesabe*: international fast food is a thing of the past. Make sure you try Tenerife's traditional cuisine.

GO GOFIO

For millennia, the Canary Islands' staple has been ▶ *gofio*, a flour made of roasted maize, millet or barley. The grain was cultivated on terraces constructed in the mountains. Wherever water gushed through gorges, millstones ground flour. This yellow or light brown powder is a filling and versatile protein-rich food – and it combines well with a wide variety of flavours. If you see *gofio escaldado*, a *caldo* (broth) made with thickened *gofio* flour, give it a go. It's served the traditional way with raw red onion slices. Today, innovative chefs even mix finely ground *gofio* with ice cream and banana purée – a daring, but very tasty creation.

A BOWL OF SOUP, SIR?

Soups and stews are very popular. Freshly prepared *sopas* are served at almost every restaurant that specialises in local cuisine. One particularly good speciality is *potaje canario*, a hearty vegetable soup.

If you think cress is only good for egg sandwiches, then you must try cress soup! This classic dish is made using large-leaved wild cress which is spicier than its farmed cousin. Traditionally, *potaje de berros* is served in a wooden bowl and garnished with half a corn on the cob.

INSIDER TIP
Eat like the locals

PICKLES & PRESERVES

For *Tinerfeños* survival has always depended on the optimum use of their resources. They tended sheep and goats and later began to hunt rabbits. But meat and fish remained a

Cress soup served with *papas arrugadas* (left), traditional *gofio* bread and cheese (right)

luxury that, until the 20th century, few islanders could afford.

Food had to be dried or preserved in salt to stop it going off, so the islanders developed a speciality known as *adobos*. Food was pickled for weeks, sometimes months, in hot sauces made from oil, vinegar, bay leaf, herbs, garlic and pepper; only then did its typical flavour develop.

LIFE WITHOUT LEFTOVERS

Leftovers as we understand them today did not exist in the past. Anything left uneaten went into stews with names like *ropa vieja* (old clothes) – an appetising reference to its recycled contents. Today, *ropa vieja*, *puchero* and *rancho canario*, meat and vegetable stews, are freshly prepared with pork, chickpeas, potatoes, pasta, onions, saffron, garlic and spicy chorizo. These are among the tastiest — and most traditional — dishes Tenerife has to offer.

Ingredients from every corner of the globe have been incorporated into the local cuisine: fennel from Andalusia, yams from Africa, saffron from La Mancha, and chayote from Latin America. A good reminder that for 400 years the Canary Islands were the meeting point of three continents.

WRINKLY POTATOES ...

The most traditional side dish is *papas arrugadas*. The famous "wrinkly potatoes", much-loved by tourists, are served in every restaurant. They are a special variety: small, dark on the outside, yellow inside. The potatoes are normally accompanied by *mojo*, a red or green spicy sauce.

FISH – GRILLED ON A PLATE

Fish and seafood is, of course, on every menu in Tenerife. Normally

Finally, every meal is rounded off with a *cortado* or a *solo* — an espresso with or without milk.

GOOD ACCOMPANIMENTS

Locals will drink Tenerife's dry lager, Dorada, or a bottle of the island's wine with their food. Tenerife is the biggest wine producer in the Canary Islands. Cultivation started shortly after the *Conquista* and, before long, many barrels were being exported back to Europe. But the colonial rivalry between Spain and England destroyed what was a thriving trade.

Vine diseases caused further damage to the island's wine industry. The tide turned only after Spain joined the EU; money from Brussels was invested in agriculture and the *Tinerfeños* began to rediscover their local tipples. Family wineries were modernised, new bodegas were opened and before long wines from Tenerife were winning international prizes.

Today on Tenerife there are five *Denominaciones de Origen* (Protected Designation of Origin). Grapes are harvested in September, so that young wine can be drunk by early November – when wine festivals take place in Icod de los Vinos, Puerto de la Cruz and Tacoronte. The best place to taste the island's vintages is the *Casa del Vino* (see p. 82) in El Sauzal. Tastings are cheap and generous!

Tenerife's wine – both red and white – is well worth trying

grilled on a hot metal plate *a la plancha*, the tastiest options include *cherne*, *sama*, *caballa* and *bocinegro*. All of these are local fish and, once lightly grilled and served with salad and *mojo*, the depth of their flavour is revealed. Two types of octopus, *pulpo* and *choco*, are also extremely popular.

FABULOUS FINALE

Every meal needs a good ending. A huge variety of fruit, from apricots to mangos and guavas, is grown on the Canary Islands. These are often served with the ubiquitous *flan* or set custard.

However, the best Canarian dessert has to be *bienmesabe* (which translates as "it tastes good to me"), a blend of honey, lemon, almonds and egg yolks.

EATING & DRINKING

Today's Menu

Starters

CALDO DE PESCADO
Fish soup with potatoes and herbs

POTAJE CANARIO
Chickpea, potato and vegetable soup

POTAJE DE BERROS
Cress soup with squash, potatoes and sweetcorn

Mains

CHERNE AL CILANTRO
Sea bream in a coriander sauce

SANCOCHO CANARIO
Saltfish stew with vegetables and sweet potato

CONEJO AL SALMOREJO
Pan-fried rabbit marinated in bay leaves, garlic and wine

CARNE DE CABRA/ BAIFO EN ADOBO
Goat in a spicy sauce

Side dishes

MOJO ROJO
Spicy chilli sauce with oil, garlic, vinegar and salt

MOJO VERDE
A milder version with coriander

PAPAS ARRUGADAS
Potatoes boiled in brine whose skin has begun to wrinkle (*arrugado* in Spanish)

GOFIO ESCALDADO
Roasted grain flour mixed with fish stock to form a paste

Desserts

LECHE ASADA
A custard made of eggs, lemon zest, cinnamon and sugar

BIENMESABE
A thick dessert made with honey, almonds, egg yolks and lemons (its name means "it tastes good to me")

FLAN CASERO
A home-made set custard

SHOPPING

From shopping outlets to luxury boutiques and farmers' markets – *Tinerfeños* love to shop and there's plenty on offer.

LOCAL FAVOURITES

Tinerfeños shop in Santa Cruz, which not only has the huge *El Corte Inglés* department store but also a range of smaller boutiques. In the old town, *Calle del Castillo* is home to a variety of global brands from Desigual to Zara. The smaller streets leading off it have some more interesting, less internationally recognisable shops. The market, *Mercado Nuestra Señora de África*, is piled high with fruit and there is a flea market *(rastro)* around it on Sundays.

For food and drink – and a great atmosphere – the 🌿 farmers' markets *(mercadillos de agricultor)* are the best choice. These are held at weekends in places like Tacoronte, where local farmers, beekeepers and winemakers come to sell their wares.

BLOOMING GREAT SOUVENIRS

One delightful souvenir is the exotic bird of paradise plant *(strelitzia)*, which grows on Tenerife. Alternatively, you can purchase a bag of *drago* seeds and plant dragon trees at home (but first check your country's import restrictions)!

WHEEL OF TIME

Alfarería – bowls, plates, jugs and drinking vessels – have always been essential basic commodities for everyday life. Today it is their simplicity that gives them their special appeal. In the village of Arguayo, near Santiago del Teide, pottery is still made using

Feast your eyes and palate: *mojo sauce* (left) and *strelitzie* or bird of paradise flower (right)

traditional methods. Without using a wheel, the potters coil the clay and the natural umber, rust red or black of the vessels is left unpainted.

Arguayo is not the only place selling ceramics; there is also a chain of state-run shops, *Artenerife (artenerife.com)*, which ensures that makers get a fair price. They have shops in Santa Cruz, La Orotaya, Playa de las Américas and Los Cristianos.

HEIGHT OF FASHION

Gran Canaria is home to the Moda Cálida brand and, not wanting to be left behind, Tenerife now has a label of its own: Tenerife Moda *(tenerife moda.com)*, whose designers are supported by the island's government. Some have made it onto the international stage, such as *Noemi Felipe*'s beachwear, elaborately embroidered fabrics from *Martina (obradoirode martina.com)*, unusual hats from *By Loleiro (byloleiro.com)* and luxurious dresses from *Mado Vigarok (mado vigarok.com)*. Tenerife Moda organises events to promote the brand, the most famous of which is the annual *Feria de la Moda* in April.

INCREDIBLE MEMORIES

Many people think food is the best souvenir. And the Canary Islands offer a great selection including world-class cheese from happy goats, the delicious *bienmesabe* almond dessert, liqueurs made from palm juice or bananas and locally made cakes. *Gofio* (see p. 26) can be bought in every supermarket or directly from one of Tenerife's last working flour mills in La Orotava.

SPORT & ACTIVITIES

With trade winds from the northeast sweeping along Tenerife's coasts, it is no surprise that windsurfing is the most popular water sport on the island. Bodyboarding off Playa de las Américas and Puerto de la Cruz has become very popular too.

There are also plenty of land-based activities – from trail running to hiking, biking, climbing, paragliding and golf… Agencies in the resort towns rent equipment and offer courses at all levels.

When it is cold in northern Europe, lots of pro sportspeople come to Tenerife to train. If you want to join them, the *T3 Athletic Sphere (daily 8am–10pm | La Caleta | Av. de los Acantillados s/n | tel. 922 78 27 55 | tenerifetoptraining.com)*, high above La Caleta/Costa Adeje, has facilities for almost any sport you care to think of, from beach volleyball to swimming (the Olympic-size pool has underwater cameras to help you analyse your performance). And there's a luxurious spa for relaxing.

The island's biggest sporting event, the *Vuelta Ciclista* – round-the-island cycle race – takes place in September.

CLIMBING PARK

At *Forestal Park Tenerife (admission 24 euros, children 12 and under 15 euros | El Rosario | forestalparktenerife. es)*, a ropes course in a pine forest in the island's north, you can test your climbing skills. Ziplines up to 200m long and platforms 30m up in the air will give you a real rush.

CYCLING

Tenerife has become very popular among professional road racers because of its steep roads and the mild winter climate. However, amateurs will find flat roads by the coast

Mountain bikers will have a great time on Tenerife's trails

(although they will have to put up with a lot of traffic). Please note: helmets are compulsory for cyclists in Spain. Mountain-bikers are allowed to go off-road.

If you're in a holiday resort, hiring a bike for a day will cost from 18 euros (weekly hire charges are discounted). *Bike Point Tenerife (Av. Quinto Centenario s/n, Playa de las Américas | tel. 922 79 67 10 | bikepointtenerife.com)* is a good supplier, with additional branches in El Médano and Callao Salvaje.

Guided bike tours, such as those led by *Ride Base (ridebasetenerife.com)* in Puerto de la Cruz cost from 50 euros (including bike hire).

DIVING

Many diving schools offer courses and trips to some amazing underwater sites – not too far from the coast. Snorkelers exploring the inshore waters will catch a glimpse of a few small fish, but scuba divers will be able to see barracudas, parrot fish, mantas, tuna and, if they're lucky, whales and dolphins. Solo diving is forbidden.

The *Centro de Buceo Atlantik (tel. 922 36 2801 | tenerife-buceo.com)* in Puerto de la Cruz runs dives from 42 euros (plus mandatory equipment hire at 27 euros per day). In Playa de las Américas, the *Aqua-Marina Dive Centre (Paseo Verode s/n (behind Hotel Oro) | tel. 678 66 26 70 | aquamarina.com)* is recommended. In Playa Paraíso, the *Paradise Dive Center (tel. 922 74 09 61 | paradisedivers.co.uk)* offers a wide range of tours, as does *Divería (Plaza 12 | tel. 649 95 70 49 | diveria.net)* in Alcalá.

GOLF

Golfers can tee off year round on three 27-hole, four 18-hole and two 9-hole golf courses. All charge a green fee but are open to the public (you can find details under Sport & activities in the regional chapters of this book).

PARAGLIDING ✓
Float above volcanoes and come down to land on white sands.  A pro will be strapped to you while you fly like a bird above mountains and valleys. There are no fewer than 40 take-off points on the island. The best one, *Izaña*, is on the Cumbre Dorsal near the observatory, at a height of 2,350m. Lots of companies offer tandem flights, equipment hire and various courses, including *Tenerfly (flights from 90 euros | C/ Reykjavik | Adeje | tel. 616 31 54 00 | tenerfly.com)*.

RIDING
Several *fincas* specialise in riding holidays. The *Finca Estrella (Fuente de Vega 24 | tel. 922 81 43 82 | teneriffa reiten.com)* near Icod de los Vinos offers hacks in the unspoilt woodland nearby.

SURFING
There are excellent surfing opportunities on the north coast; however, the best place is *Playa de Benijo*, beyond the Anaga Mountains, although it can take a long time to get there. A good spot for beginners is *Playa de Martiánez* in Puerto de la Cruz. More experienced surfers are well served at *Playa del Socorro* or *Playa Punta Brava*, west of Puerto de la Cruz. Conditions are also ideal off *El Médano* in the south. There is a surf school in Puerto de la Cruz at Playa Martiánez *(lamareasurfschool.com)*.

WALKING
The most beautiful hiking areas include *Valle de La Orotava*, the *Anaga* and *Teno* mountain ranges and

Hiking in Parque Nacional del Teide

SPORT & ACTIVITIES

Surfers get their kicks on the Atlantic swell

Parque Nacional del Teide. And in the south, there is the enticing *Barranco del Infierno*. Most trails are well signposted but the terrain is often steep so make sure you're well prepared and in good physical shape before you set off. Inexperienced hikers can join a 🌿 guided walk. There are plenty to pick from, including *Sergio Walking Tours (sergiowalkingtours.com)*; Sergio also leads tours from a four-star hotel in the quiet village of *Los Silos (Luz del Mar | Av. Sibora 10 | La Caleta | tel. 922 84 16 23 | luzdelmar.de/en | €€)*. The hotel is perfectly located to explore the countryside and offers tours at all levels or you can hire maps and GPS phones if you prefer to explore alone.

The big resorts all have agencies offering English-speaking guides and tours at differing levels.

**INSIDER TIP
A hiker's paradise**

WINDSURFING

The hot spots are mainly along Tenerife's southeast coast. With wind strengths in winter usually around 5, in summer as high as 8, experienced windsurfers love it here. *El Cabezo* and *La Jaquita* (wind strengths 4–8) are only suitable for experts. World championship events are staged in the inshore waters near *El Médano* (wind strengths 3–5).

The Surf Center (C/ La Gaviota | tel. 642 85 09 05 | surfcenter.eu) offers wind- and kitesurfing courses at all levels. They also hire boards and offer storage if you have your own board. The more sheltered conditions off *Playa de las Américas* and along the west coast are perfect for novices.

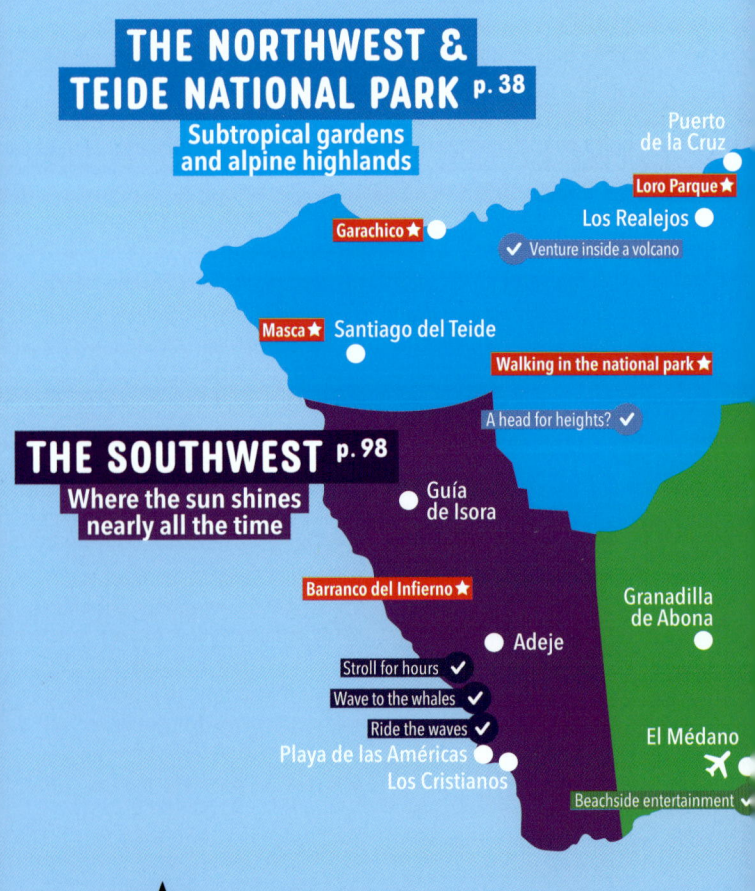

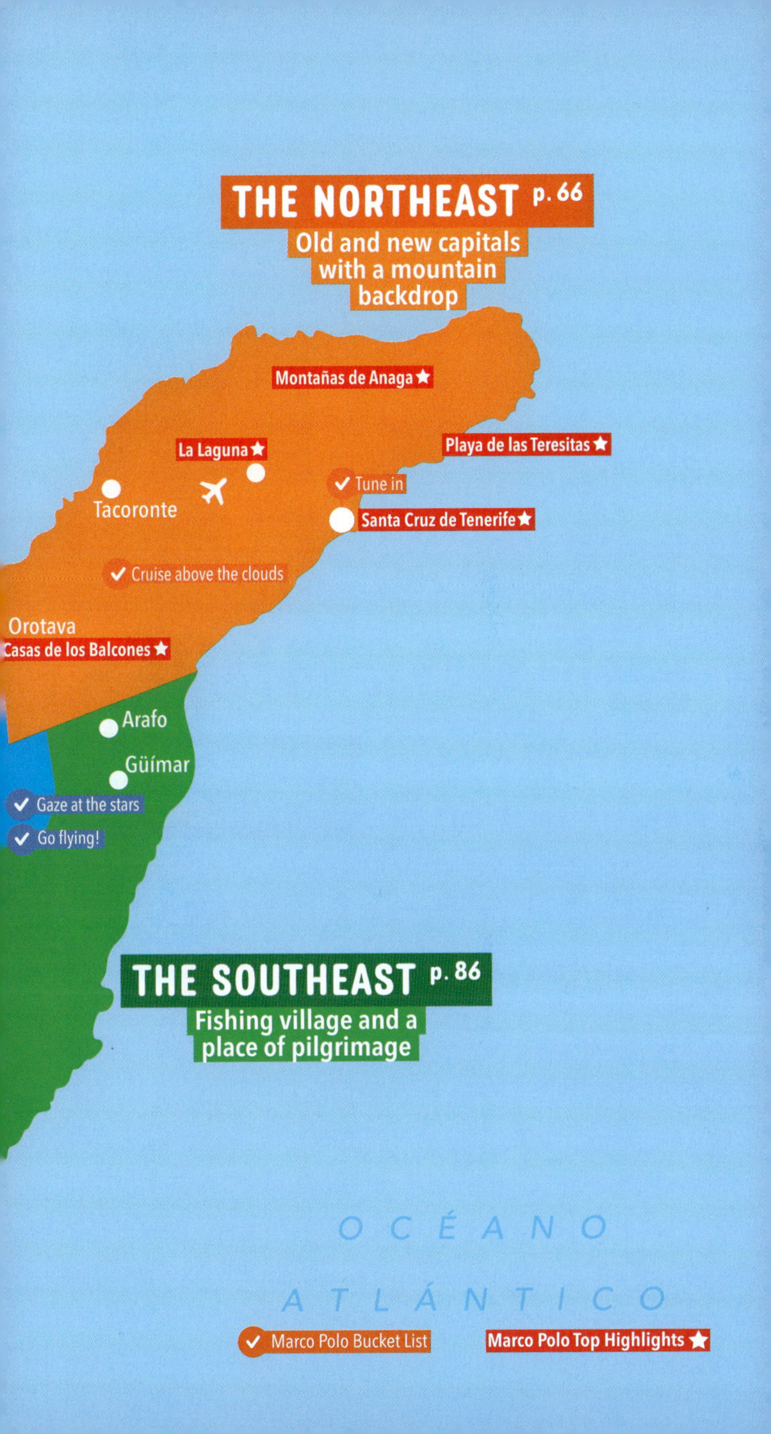

THE NORTHEAST p. 66
Old and new capitals with a mountain backdrop

- Montañas de Anaga ★
- La Laguna ★
- Playa de las Teresitas ★
- Tacoronte
- ✓ Tune in
- Santa Cruz de Tenerife ★
- ✓ Cruise above the clouds
- Orotava
- Casas de los Balcones ★
- Arafo
- Güímar
- ✓ Gaze at the stars
- ✓ Go flying!

THE SOUTHEAST p. 86
Fishing village and a place of pilgrimage

OCÉANO ATLÁNTICO

✓ Marco Polo Bucket List   ★ Marco Polo Top Highlights

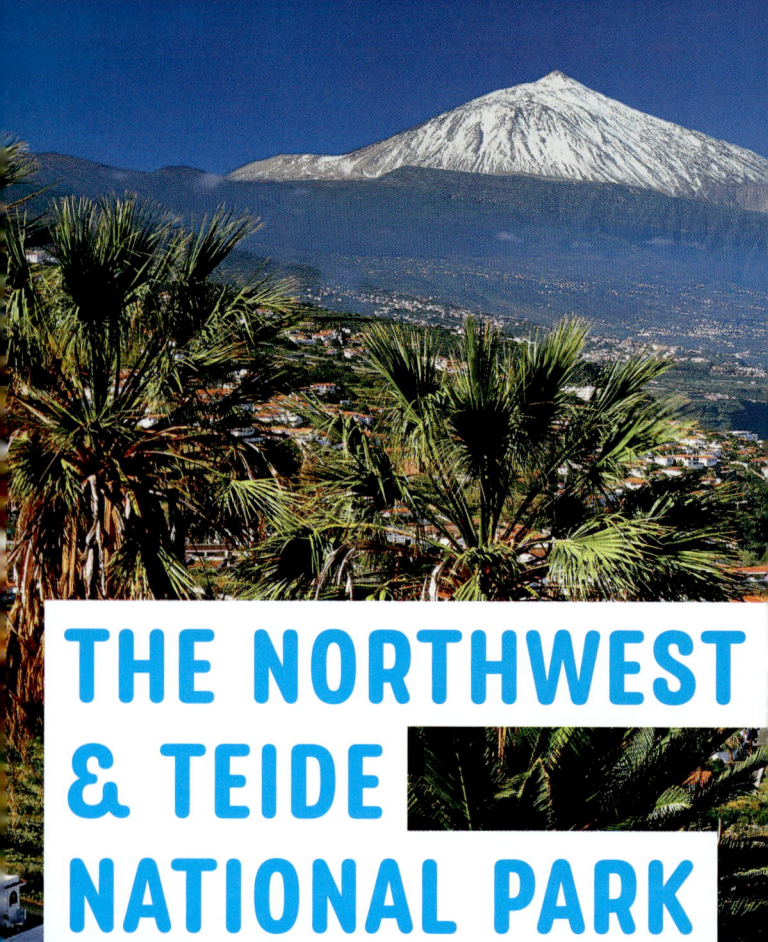

THE NORTHWEST & TEIDE NATIONAL PARK

VERDANT VALLEYS & SPAIN'S HIGHEST PEAK

Nowhere else on Tenerife has such a varied landscape as the northwest. Valle de La Orotava is the island's greenest spot thanks to the trade winds, which keep it well supplied with moisture.

When he first set eyes on the valley in 1799, the German explorer, Alexander von Humboldt, wrote "… I have never beheld a prospect more varied, more attractive, more harmonious in the distribution of the masses of verdure and rocks".

Mount Teide rises above the Orotava Valley

The valley is no longer so remote. Tourism has brought income but also overdevelopment. Around the northern resort of Puerto de la Cruz ugly hotels blot the coast. However, the further west you go, the more you leave these eyesores behind. In small villages in the shadow of Pico del Teide, farmers tend their crops and goats or cultivate vines as they have for centuries, while the rugged Teno Mountains to the west are a spectacular sight.

THE NORTHWEST & TEIDE NATIONAL PARK

MARCO POLO HIGHLIGHTS

★ **GARACHICO**
Historic old town, wild and windswept coast, a castle and good restaurants
➤ p. 56

★ **MASCA**
A stunning village built of mountain stone lies hidden between rugged cliffs ➤ p. 61

★ **DRAGO MILENARIO**
Icod de los Vinos is home to what is reputedly the oldest dragon tree in the world ➤ p. 54

★ **CASAS DE LOS BALCONES**
La Orotava's grand houses have delightful patios that are well worth admiring
➤ p. 51

★ **JARDÍN BOTÁNICO**
Exotic plants from all over the world in Puerto de la Cruz's botanical garden
➤ p. 44

★ **PLAYA JARDÍN**
Black sand with palms, waterfalls and little rockpools ➤ p. 48

A blanket of cloud often covers the north of Tenerife. It means the climate here is pleasantly fresh and moist and the landscape is greener than anywhere else on the island.

MARCO POLO BUCKET LIST

3 ✓ Gaze at the stars
Look directly into space from the *Observatorio del Teide* ➤ p. 65

4 ✓ Go flying!
Paraglide from the mountains and land on the beach ➤ p. 34

6 ✓ A head for heights?
The *Teide cable car* transports you over a surreal barren landscape ➤ p. 64

8 ✓ Venture inside a volcano
The *Cueva del Viento* is one of the longest lava tunnels in the world ➤ p. 56

★ **LORO PARQUE**
See more than just *loros* (parrots):
dolphins, seals and even orcas ➤ p. 45

★ **CORPUS CHRISTI**
Carpets made from volcanic sand are
created in La Orotava to celebrate the
festival of Corpus Christi ➤ p. 54

★ **WALKING**
The unique natural world at Las Cañadas
in the national park will take your
breath away ➤ p. 65

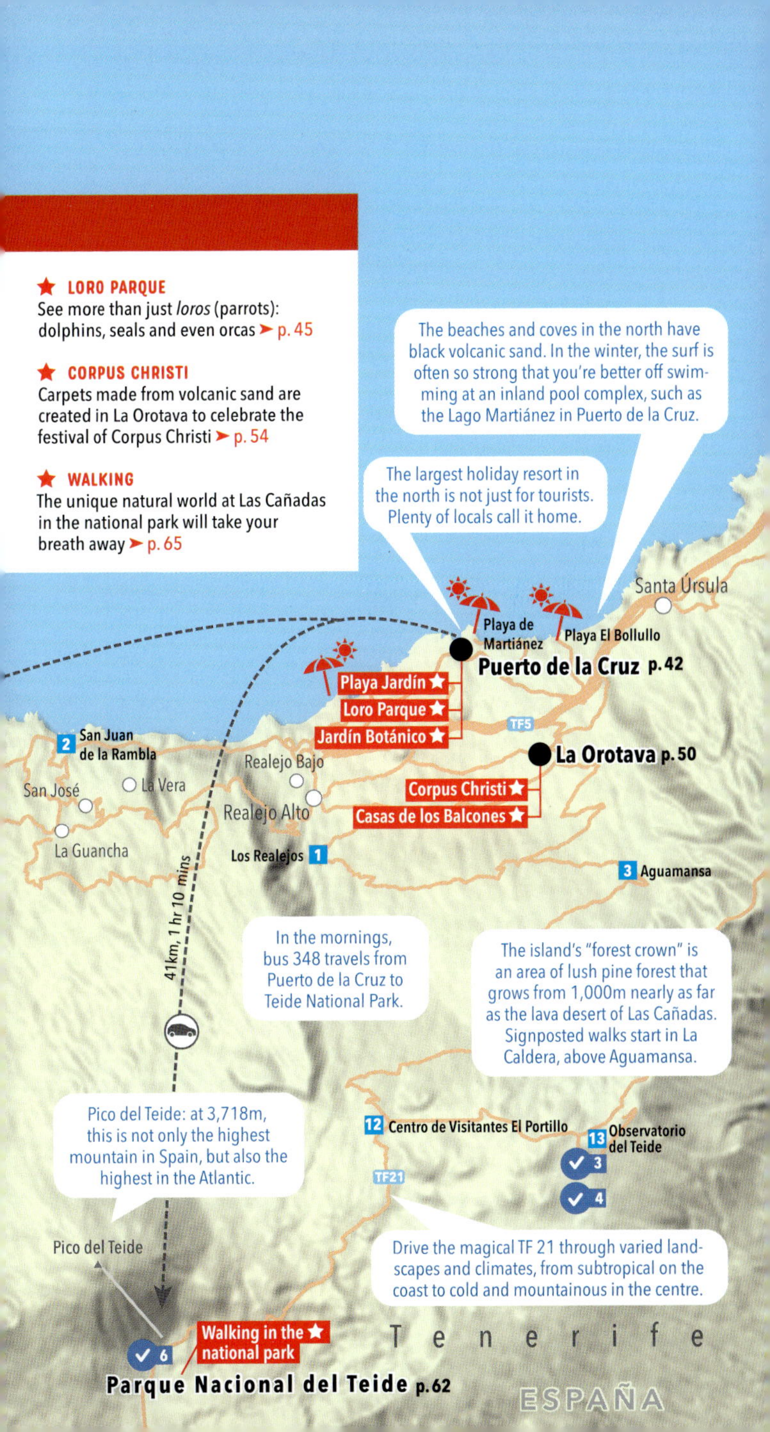

The beaches and coves in the north have black volcanic sand. In the winter, the surf is often so strong that you're better off swimming at an inland pool complex, such as the Lago Martiánez in Puerto de la Cruz.

The largest holiday resort in the north is not just for tourists. Plenty of locals call it home.

Santa Úrsula

Playa de Martiánez   Playa El Bollullo
● **Puerto de la Cruz** p. 42

Playa Jardín ★
Loro Parque ★
Jardín Botánico ★

San Juan de la Rambla 2

Realejo Bajo   TF5   ● **La Orotava** p. 50
San José   ○ La Vera
Realejo Alto   **Corpus Christi** ★
                   Casas de los Balcones ★
La Guancha

Los Realejos 1   3 Aguamansa

In the mornings, bus 348 travels from Puerto de la Cruz to Teide National Park.

The island's "forest crown" is an area of lush pine forest that grows from 1,000m nearly as far as the lava desert of Las Cañadas. Signposted walks start in La Caldera, above Aguamansa.

41km, 1 hr 10 mins

Pico del Teide: at 3,718m, this is not only the highest mountain in Spain, but also the highest in the Atlantic.

12 Centro de Visitantes El Portillo   13 Observatorio del Teide
TF21   ✓ 3
                    ✓ 4

Pico del Teide
▲

Drive the magical TF 21 through varied landscapes and climates, from subtropical on the coast to cold and mountainous in the centre.

T e n e r i f e

✓ 6   **Walking in the national park** ★

Parque Nacional del Teide p. 62

ESPAÑA

PUERTO DE LA CRUZ

PUERTO DE LA CRUZ

(📖 F-G3) **Huge ugly buildings are surrounded by lush parks, crowded streets, bright swimming pools, seedy neon signs and grand colonial buildings, and old men pass the time of day on grand plazas. Puerto de la Cruz struggles to find the right balance between the past and the present and is still working out how best to manage its tourism business.**

By 1900, the British had discovered this cool spot and its pleasant climate and claimed it for themselves. The first hotels were built in grand gardens above the fishing village, which until then had been used by the Spanish as a port for exporting sugar cane and wine from the Orotava Valley.

THE NORTHWEST & TEIDE NATIONAL PARK

There were elegant hotels like the casino hotel Taoro, which still sits proudly above the town, and re-opened as a five-star hotel in 2024. Many Canary islanders only settled here once tourism had become established; since the 1960s the spa hotels have been joined by huge hotel complexes and guesthouses.

Unlike the resorts in the south, locals and tourists have to rub along here, and the town does its best to meet the needs of its 45,000 inhabitants as well as the demands of the hundreds of thousands of holidaymakers who flock here each year. Between Playa de Martiánez in the east and Plaza del Charco in the centre, you will find many shops, restaurants and modern glass office buildings, as well as examples of colonial architecture and squares to relax in.

PUERTO DE LA CRUZ

WHERE TO START?

The nicest bits of Puerto are down at the water's edge and on its "second floor" around the **Parque Taoro**. As the town sprawls for several kilometres along the coast, it is worth making sure you take the right exit *(salida)* from the TF-5 motorway: Salida 32 for the *Jardín Botánico* and *La Paz* area; Salida 35 for *Parque Taoro*; Salida 35 or 36 for *Playa Jardín*; Salida 39 for *Loro Parque*. Caution: there are not many car parks but there is an underground one at the *Centro Comercial Pirámides de Martiánez* (Salida 32).

SIGHTSEEING

CASA DE LA REAL ADUANA

One of the oldest buildings in Puerto de la Cruz is the Royal Customs House. Built in 1620, its wooden windows and balconies perfectly exemplify Canarian architecture. It ceased to function as a customs house 150 years ago. Now the ground floor of the building houses a tourist office and *Artenerife* shop selling local handicrafts, while the upstairs is home to the *Museum of Contemporary Art (MACEW)*, which shows work by Canarian artists, including some particularly expressive local painters like Juan Ismael and surrealist Óscar Domínguez. *Mon–Sat 10am–2pm | admission 2 euros | C/ Las Lonjas 1 | ⏱ 30 mins*

> **INSIDER TIP**
> Beautifully odd

CASA MUSEO DEL PESCADOR

This "fisherman's house" is jam-packed with model ships, stuffed fish and a host of skeletons, as well as old photos of life on the high seas. *Daily 9am–7pm | admission free | C/ las Lonjas 5 | ⏱ 30 mins*

CASTILLO SAN FELIPE

San Felipe castle is just under 1km from the centre of town. It was built between 1630 and 1644 to defend the island from pirates, hence the intimidating cannon by the entrance. The building is now used for cultural events and exhibitions. There's a huge rockery and a view over Playa Jardín. *Tue–Sat 11am–1pm and 5–8pm | admission free | Paseo de Luis Lavaggi | ⏱ 30 mins*

IGLESIA DE NUESTRA SEÑORA DE LA PEÑA DE FRANCIA

Built in 1697, Puerto's main church is situated on the elevated *Plaza de la Iglesia*. It has a heavily gilded altarpiece on the Baroque main altar and stunning statues of several saints, including the *Virgen del Rosario* and the *Virgen de los Dolores*. *C/ Quintana*

JARDÍN BOTÁNICO ★

Tropical plants of every kind. Cinnamon trees, sausage trees, strangler figs, pepper and tulip trees, coral and breadfruit trees, coffee and cocoa bushes, araucaria, various fruit trees and a fig tree as tall as a church – you can see all of this and much more at the botanical garden. It was built by King Carlos III in 1790 on some 2 hectares of land to help exotic plants

THE NORTHWEST & TEIDE NATIONAL PARK

Art and culture are protected behind the thick walls of Castillo San Felipe

from the tropics adjust to the temperate climate of Europe. The second stage of this ambitious plan, i.e. to introduce these plants to the Spanish mainland, was less successful as plants that flourished in tropical climates did not like the cool winters of Madrid. *Daily 9am–6pm | admission 3 euros | C/ Retama 2 | 1 hr*

LAGO MARTIÁNEZ

César Manrique, the brilliant landscape architect from Lanzarote, designed a 100,000m² swimming area here between the cliffs with waterfalls, fountains and big seawater swimming pools all set in green surroundings. *Daily 10am–5pm | admission 5.50 euros, children (up to 10) 2.50 euros | Costa Martiánez | lago martianez.com*

LORO PARQUE ★

The biggest zoo on the Canary Islands. With everything from gorillas to lions and Bengal tigers, there is plenty to see here. In the huge bird enclosures, there are rope bridges and ladders allowing you to get close to the animals. A vast, snow-filled dome houses two different species of penguin and there is an aquarium in a tunnel meaning you can get very close to over 20,000 species of fish, sharks and rays. And there are dolphin, sea lion and orca shows every day. While young visitors love the opportunity to get up close and personal with the underwater creatures, animal rights' campaigners argue that no aquarium can ever replicate the thousands of kilometres travelled by these animals in their natural ocean habitat. Ultimately, this is true of any animal in

PUERTO DE LA CRUZ

captivity and is the argument used to support the abolition of zoos. That said, Loro Parque contributes to environmental and animal protection projects and provides funding for related scientific research. If you want to find out more about Loro Parque's work and about what goes on behind the scenes of the zoo, book a Loro Explore Tour. *Daily 9.30am–5.30pm (last entry) | admission 42 euros, children (5–11) 28 euros, under-5s free (Loro Explore Tour 15/10 euros extra); combined ticket with Siam Park 74/53 euros; shuttle-service from holiday resorts in the south of the island (advance bookings only 19/14 euros) | Playa Punta Brava | free mini-train every 20 mins from Playa de Martiánez | loroparque.com | 4–5 hrs*

INSIDER TIP For the full experience ...

MUSEO ARQUEOLÓGICO MUNICIPAL
On the west side of the Plaza del Charco stands the town's Archaeological Museum with a collection of Guanche mummies, weapons and historical maps. *Mon–Fri 9am–3pm | admission free | C/ del Lomo 9a*

PARQUE TAORO
The first grand hotels were built for mainly British spa guests at the end of the 19th century on this plateau overlooking the sea and the town. The park covers 10 hectares and consists of gardens, footpaths, lookouts, waterfalls, fountains, a playground and a restaurant. Within the grounds, behind the former Taoro Casino Hotel, is a beautiful, if somewhat overgrown, terraced garden. Known as the *Risco Bello*, it boasts a fine array of flowers, fruits, an ivy-covered grotto and a *Jardín Acuático* with plenty of ponds. *Altos de Taoro*

PUERTO PESQUERO
You will be greeted at this narrow fishing harbour by the *Pescadora*, a life-size bronze statue of a woman carrying a basket on her head. When the boats arrive back in port, buyers emerge amid a bustle of activity and the noisy haggling over the day's catch begins.

Enjoy a glass of wine in the Templo del Vino

THE NORTHWEST & TEIDE NATIONAL PARK

EATING & DRINKING

BAMBI GOURMET
Hidden away in a side street, yet always busy with a cosy atmosphere, Bambi Gourmet serves a variety of freshly made European dishes – from salmon moussaka to porcini mushroom risotto – and Romanian specialities, such as veal cheek goulash. Great desserts! *Daily 1–10pm | C/ Enrique Talg 15 | tel. 822 90 28 36 | €€*

CAFÉ ALBA
Tuck into snacks, salads and cakes with a stunning view of the coast. Their home-made lemonade is delicious. Curiously, on the way there, at *Mirador La Paz*, you will come across a statue of Agatha Christie. *C/ Pitera 5 | tel. 922 37 10 54 | €*

CASA RÉGULO
Imaginative, multiple award-winning Canarian cuisine in a renovated mansion. Try the octopus carpaccio *(carpaccio de pulpo). Tue–Sat 12.30–3pm and 6–10pm | C/ Pérez Zamora 16 | tel. 922 38 45 06 | €€€*

EL TEMPLO DEL VINO
A near religious drinking (and eating) experience: exquisite Canarian wines served with delicious tapas. If you are very hungry, order a kebab which comes served (ominously) "on the gallows" with spicy sauces! *Daily 1–11pm | C/ del Lomo 2 | tel. 922 37 41 64 | templodelvino.com | €€*

SHOPPING

CALLE QUINTANA
You'll find everything – from art galleries to supermarkets – in the pedestrianised heart of the old town. The old-fashioned *Columbus Plaza* shopping centre has an attractive patio and shops selling everything from the latest fashions to cigars and perfumes.

MERCADO MUNICIPAL
The concrete market hall is not a pretty sight. But it still attracts many shoppers looking for fresh local produce. If you're craving good seafood, visit *Tasca el Cayuco* upstairs. There is also a flea market here on Wednesdays and Saturdays 10am–2pm. *Mon–Sat 8am–2pm and 4–8pm | C/ Blas Pérez González 6 | mercadomunicipal.net*

SPORT & ACTIVITIES

CYCLING
If you want to get around Puerto de la Cruz by bicycle, you can hire mountain bikes, e-bikes and trekking bikes or join a guided tour. Whichever is your preferred option, you'll find it at *Ride Base (Av. Francisco Afonso Carillo/ Ed. Playa Bahía II | tel. 650 51 38 59 | ridebasetenerife.com | mountain-bike from 30 euros/day)* on Playa Jardín.

HIKING
Puerto de la Cruz is a good starting point for walking tours of the national park. Bus 348 runs to El Portillo visitor centre, Teide cable car and the *Parador* each morning. Lots of organisations offer guided walks.

PUERTO DE LA CRUZ

LEARN SOME SPANISH
The boutique hotel *Puerto Azul* is attached to *Sothis Language School (C/ del Lomo 24 | tel. 922 38 32 13 | sothis.es)* where you can take courses at all levels and intensities.

INSIDER TIP Hablas español?

WELLNESS

ORIENTAL SPA GARDEN
Puerto's nicest spa is the *Hotel Botánico*'s Oriental Garden. It welcomes non-residents and has thalasso pools alongside jacuzzis outside, and a range of saunas, steam rooms, flotation tanks and therapeutic showers in a series of caves inside. All set in a pretty garden with a fishpond and pagoda. *Daily 9am–8pm | C/ Richard J Yeoward 1 | treatments from 45 euros | tel. 922 38 95 05 | orientalspagarden.com*

BEACHES

PLAYA EL BOLLULLO
This 200m-long, pitch-black beach is hidden away beneath steep picturesque cliffs 4km to the east of Puerto de la Cruz.

PLAYA DE MARTIÁNEZ
The almost untouched town beach (250m long) to the east of Puerto de la Cruz is composed of coarse, black sand with outcrops of volcanic rock. There's a boardwalk for walkers and the view along the north coast is incredible.

PLAYA JARDÍN ★
It is called "Garden Beach" for a reason. With a waterpark, lush tropical flora, and lots of caves, this is a charming spot. It looks so pretty and natural that it's hard to believe it is artificial – they had to bring in 200,000m³ of volcanic sand, as well as build an underwater reef to stop the sand being washed away. There are lots of cafés and restaurants catering to your every need. In summer 2024, the beach suffered from a damaged sewage pipe and poor water quality; fortunately, this has since been fixed.

NIGHTLIFE

Plaza del Charco is a popular spot, with bars, cafés and ice cream parlours. The *Compostela Club Café (daily)* is a wonderfully retro, tropical and chilled bar, with lots of tables and a good selection of drinks. Around the corner, the rustic *Bodega Julián (C/ Mequinez 20 | tel. 686 55 63 15 | €€)* serves good food to the sound of live Latin American and Spanish music.

Night owls will inevitably find themselves heading towards Lago de Martiánez. *Café de París (Av. de Colón 2)* has a terrace and serves cocktails until midnight. Things only get lively after midnight and at weekends in the area around *Calle La Hoya* and the intersecting *Av. Familia Betancourt y Molina*.

If you feel the need to boost your holiday funds, you can always try your luck at the *casino (Tue–Sat 7pm–2am, Sun and Thu 8pm–3am | Av. de Colón | admission free (bring some ID) | tel. 922 38 05 50 | casinostenerife.com)*.

THE NORTHWEST & TEIDE NATIONAL PARK

AROUND PUERTO DE LA CRUZ

1 LOS REALEJOS
10km/10 mins southwest of Puerto de la Cruz on the TF-333

West of Puerto de la Cruz, the municipality of Los Realejos is an amalgamation of several small villages spread over steep ridges and separated by deep canyons. Tenerife's first church (1496) *Santiago Apóstol*, is testimony to this area's former wealth – today's testaments are large hotels.

Beneath the village of La Guancha you can visit *Bodegas Viñátigo (Mon–Fri 8.30am–5.30pm | guided tours by appointment only 11am Mon, Wed and Fri 35 euros | 1.5km from La Guancha on TF-352, C/ Travesía Juandana | bodegas vinatigo.com)*. This modern winery has used beautiful natural stone to create a stunning tasting room.

INSIDER TIP
A stylish place to sip

In the neighbourhood of La Montañeta, close to Puerto de la Cruz, a former monastery has been converted into a restaurant, *El Monasterio (daily noon–midnight | La Vera, C/ La Montañeta | tel. 922 34 07 07 |*

Playa Jardín: the black-sand "garden beach" of Puerto de la Cruz at the foot of Mount Teide

LA OROTAVA

mesonelmonasterio.com | €–€€), Small animals roam freely in the landscaped monastery grounds. Choose between traditional Canarian cuisine in the formal restaurant and snacks in the bodega. *F4*

2 SAN JUAN DE LA RAMBLA
14km/17 mins west of Puerto de la Cruz on the TF-5
It won't take long to walk through all the alleys of this historic, somewhat sleepy town. More excitement can be found in the fishermen's quarter *Las Aguas*, where waves incessantly pound against the cliffs. It's not only nice to look at, it'll also awaken your appetite, which you can satisfy at *Las Aguas (daily 1–3.30pm, Wed–Sat 7–10pm | C/ La Destila 20 | tel. 922 36 04 28 | €€)*, a restaurant located in a country house above the promenade. *E3*

LA OROTAVA

(*G3*) **Grand town houses line steep narrow lanes, while elegant mansions with spacious, dark-wood balconies surround large squares. La Orotava is one of the oldest towns in the Canary Islands.**

Ignore the traffic and new housing developments on the outskirts, and you'll think you're back in colonial times! It is no surprise that, at the beginning of the 16th century, the Spaniards decided to build a town here. With water bubbling from the many springs, this was the lushest part of the green *Valle de La Orotava*, and its fertile soil provided bountiful harvests. They planted sugar cane, which was then shipped from the port, Puerto de La Orotava (now Puerto de la Cruz), all over the world, and as a result amassed considerable wealth.

Although earthquakes in 1704 and 1705 destroyed large parts of the town, it was immediately rebuilt. That explains why the historic centre remains largely intact, and it is protected as a part of Europe's cultural heritage. Tourism in *La Orotava* (pop. 40,000) is mainly restricted to day visitors strolling through the old town with its fine squares. But there's plenty of attractive accommodation, so you could stay a bit longer …

THE NORTHWEST & TEIDE NATIONAL PARK

Casas de los Balcones: wooden balconies in the patio of Casa Fonseca

SIGHTSEEING

CASAS DE LOS BALCONES ★

Plain but elegant houses face each other in *Calle San Francisco*. They get their name, *Casas de los Balcones*, from their wonderful and finely crafted wooden balconies – a typical characteristic of Canarian buildings. The balconies look as though they have been glued on to the façade. The first, *Casa Fonseca (daily 9am–6.30pm | admission 5 euros incl. audio guide | ⓘ 30 mins)*, was built in 1632, and enchants visitors with its plant-filled patio and an arcade panelled entirely with wood on the first floor. The rooms are now used by an embroidery school. The equally fine house next door, *Casa de Franchi*, was built in 1670; it now houses a carpet museum, the *Museo de las Alfombras (Mon–Fri 11am–2pm, 4–6pm | admission 3 euros | ⓘ 15 mins)*. However, these are not woven rugs but floor coverings made from volcanic sand, as seen in the Corpus Christi celebrations.

Opposite is *Casa Molina*, formerly a monastery dating from 1590. It now houses one of the island's largest craft shops, *Casa del Turista*. casa-balcones.com

CENTRO DE VISITANTES TELESFORO BRAVO DEL PARQUE

The multimedia exhibition will take you through Tenerife's geological and

LA OROTAVA

human history, from sea level to almost 4,000m and from the coast to the summit of Mount Teide – there is even "lava" flowing beneath your feet. *Tue–Sun 9am–2pm and 3.30–6pm | admission free | C/ Sixto Perera 25, El Mayorazgo, junction 34 | tel. 922 92 23 71 | reservasparquesnacionales.es*

HIJUELA DEL BOTÁNICO

The "little daughter" *(hijuela)* of the Puerto de la Cruz botanical garden is hidden behind the town hall and, at 4,000m², really is quite small. But it's still worth a visit to see the Australian conifers, Indian chestnut trees, flame trees (flamboyants) and a lovely dragon tree. Some plants date back to the foundation of the garden in 1788. *Mon–Fri 9am–6pm, Sat/Sun 10am–3pm | admission free | C/ Tomás Pérez*

JARDINES DEL MARQUESADO DE LA QUINTA ROJA

Above Hijuela del Botánico, a pretty park climbs up the terraced slope. Passing by exotic plants, each more magnificent and colourful than the one before, you will reach the Marqués de la Quinta Roja's marble mausoleum. from here, you can enjoy a panorama of the town from above. *Daily 9am–6pm | admission free*

INSIDER TIP A grave with a view

MUSEO DE ARTESANÍA IBEROAMERICANA

There is an arts and crafts museum in the former Dominican monastery of Santo Domingo, which dates from the 17th century. You will see traditional costumes, instruments and beautiful objects from Spain and the New World. The monastery's cloister is a masterpiece of simplicity. *Mon–Fri 10am–3pm, Sat 10am–2pm | admission 3 euros | C/ Tomás Zerolo 34*

PARROQUIA DE LA INMACULADA CONCEPCIÓN DE LA VIRGEN MARÍA

Less is more? Not here, where it's all about pomp! Two bell towers flank a massive, richly decorated Baroque façade. And that's just a taste of the splendour that awaits you inside. The three naves are divided by pillars and a mighty dome arches up over the crossing. It lets in just enough light to make the jasper and marble altar below shimmer mysteriously. The Church of the Immaculate Conception was consecrated to the Virgin Mary in 1788. It was meant to surpass the beauty of its predecessor destroyed in the 1704–05 earthquakes: "What the destructive forces of nature take from us, we will rebuild all the more splendidly!" *Plaza Casañas*

PLAZA DE LA CONSTITUCIÓN

The pavilion in the middle of Constitution Square is the heart of La Orotava. The square is generously proportioned and always beautifully planted with flowers and shrubs. It is surrounded by a number of historical buildings – such as *San Agustín*, a former convent dating back to 1671, and the *Liceo de Taoro*, a palace painted rust red which is now a private cultural centre. There's a great view from the

THE NORTHWEST & TEIDE NATIONAL PARK

plaza too, with the town spreading out at your feet!

PLAZA DEL AYUNTAMIENTO
La Orotava's second main square is overlooked by seven towering Canary palm trees in front of the town hall. This is the stage for all the major festivals, including the colourful Corpus Christi celebrations. Around Christmas, a beautiful life-size Nativity scene adorns one of the neighbouring streets *(C/ Isla de la Gomera 7)*.

RUTA DE LOS MOLINOS DE AGUA
No fewer than nine waterwheels were built to take advantage of La Orotava's abundance of water. Mostly dating from the 16th century, they were still being used well into the 20th century. Built in a row along streets that climbed steeply up the hillside, their job was to grind *gofio*, the Canarian staple (see p. 26). The mills were linked by channels that carried water from the Araujo stream and then from one mill to the next. Seven of the mills and parts of the channels can still be seen.

One of the three mills that are still working – *Molino de Gofio La Máquina (Calle Colegio 3)* – is now powered by electricity and continues to grind (and sell) fresh *gofio* every day. *Mon–Fri 9am–5pm, Sat 8am–2pm | start of route: south of the Casas de los Balcones*

INSIDER TIP: It tastes best fresh

The pretty pavilion on Plaza de la Constitución is the place to be in La Orotava

AROUND LA OROTAVA

EATING & DRINKING

SABOR CANARIO
"Canarian flavour" *(sabor canario)* in a historic stately home in the old town. The chefs here are passionate about traditional fare – from *rancho* to *bienmesabe*. Mon–Sat 5.30–10pm | C/ Carrera 17 | tel. 922 32 27 25 | €–€€

SHOPPING

CASA DE LOS BALCONES & CASA DEL TURISTA
These two shops sell a wide range of souvenirs and tasty delicacies. However, not everything is locally sourced. Mon–Sat 9am–6.30pm (Casa de los Balcones also Sun) | C/ San Fernando 3 and 4

CASA TORREHERMOSA
Selling certified (collector's) items made by Tenerife's artisans, the organisation *Artenerife* (Mon–Fri 10am–3pm | C/ Tomás Zerolo 27) is housed in a 17th-century mansion.

FESTIVALS

CORPUS CHRISTI ★
Carpets made from lava? At Corpus Christi you will see them on show in La Orotava's biggest festival. The huge "carpets" portray hyper-realistic biblical scenes using lots of different-coloured volcanic sand. The finest of them all are displayed at Plaza de la Constitución in front of the town hall.

AROUND LA OROTAVA

🔳 AGUAMANSA
13km/15 mins southeast of La Orotava on TF-21
Beyond the village of Aguamansa, on the way to the Parque Nacional del Teide, there is a dense pine forest where you can park up and look back up the beautiful Orotava Valley. On the left-hand side you will find a picnic spot in a crater, *La Caldera*. From there, signposted walking trails head off in all directions. 📖 *G4*

ICOD DE LOS VINOS

(📖 *E4*) **Is it crazy to visit a place because of one tree? If that's your reason for coming to Icod de los Vinos, you won't be alone. Thousands arrive every year to see the best dragon trees on the island.**

Although ★ 🚩 the *Drago Milenario* does not date back 1,000 years as the name suggests, its age is estimated at 500 to 600 years, making it the oldest dragon tree in the world. With a diameter of 6m and a height of 17m, it is also unsurpassed in size. It occupies a prominent position in the middle of town in its own botanic garden, the *Parque del Drago* (daily 9am–6pm | admission 5 euros | Plaza de la Constitución 1 | ⏱ *30 mins*). The

THE NORTHWEST & TEIDE NATIONAL PARK

garden has a "Guanche trail", where you learn about the island's original inhabitants.

Going for a stroll through Icod (pop. 23,000) can be fun too. Founded in 1501, vines were quickly planted on its fertile hills, and the local wine can be tasted and purchased in the town's many bodegas.

SIGHTSEEING

IGLESIA SAN MARCOS
The 15th-century *San Marcos* church sits on Icod's pretty main square, the *Plaza Lorenzo Cáceres*, near the Parque del Drago. Through its Renaissance portal you'll enter the dimly lit interior with its carved wooden ceiling. Make sure you take in the silver-embossed Baroque altar. Even more silver lies in the Treasury. The *Plaza de Pila* with its 18th-century houses is just a few metres away and is home to some nice wine shops.

MUSEO MUÑECAS/ARTLANDYA
The place is as eccentric and beautiful as the exhibition itself. Hundreds of dolls designed by acclaimed designers are exhibited in a colourful hacienda. You can find out how the dolls are made on a tour of the workshop. Oh, and there are teddy bears in all shapes and sizes to see too … *Thu–Sun noon–6pm | admission 10 euros | Camino el Moleiro 21, 3km to the east of Santa Bárbara | artlandya.com | ⏱ 1 hr*

INSIDER TIP
Return to childhood

The *Drago Milenario* in Icod de los Vinos

EATING & DRINKING

CARMEN
It can get fairly cool in Icod. The perfect way to get warm is with a hearty, spicy cress soup – *potaje de berros*! And the rustic atmosphere with lots of wood will warm up your heart too. *Daily noon–5pm | C/ Hércules 2 | tel. 922 81 06 31 | €€*

GARACHICO

AROUND ICOD DE LOS VINOS

4 CUEVA DEL VIENTO ✓
5km/10 mins south of Icod on the TF-366

If you want to climb into the bowels of a volcano, you've come to the right place. At a small visitor centre, you will receive an introduction into how the "cave of the wind" came into being. It was formed 27,000 years ago, when the Pico Viejo erupted and sent trails of lava flowing down into the valley. The lava cooled rapidly on the surface, while underneath it kept flowing, thereby creating tunnels. At 17km in length, this is one of the longest lava tubes in the world. In eternal darkness, only highly adaptable creatures have been able to make a home here, including a blind cockroach – don't worry, it's totally harmless! *Daily 9am–5pm, Thu until 6pm | admission 20 euros, advance booking required | 2-hr tours twice daily | C/ los Piquetes 51 | tel. 922 81 53 39 | cuevadelviento.net | sturdy shoes required |* ▭ *E4*

5 SAN MARCOS
2 km/5 mins north of Icod on the TF-414

One of the few beaches to swim at in the north.

> **INSIDER TIP**
> **A striking beach all to yourselves**

About 100m long, the beach of pitch-black volcanic sand is deserted on weekdays, but on Saturday and Sunday it fills up with hundreds of islanders who come here to swim, spend the weekend in the nearby apartments and keep the small, local restaurants busy. One of them, *Casa Chicha (Thu–Sun noon–10.30pm | tel. 922 09 11 86 | €–€€)* is on the promenade overlooking sea and beach. Their speciality — like almost everywhere else here — is fish. ▭ *E4*

GARACHICO

(▭ *D4*) **Beautiful architecture, terrific natural surroundings – ★ life is good in Garachico! Cobblestone alleys lined with historic buildings lead to a plaza with monasteries, churches and old laurel trees.**

Immediately behind, cliffs rise to heights of 1,000m, and on the volcanic coast, naturally formed pools offer a place to take a dip – don't get in unless it's calm! Garachico (pop. 5,700) is idyllic – despite a major disaster in 1706 when mighty streams of lava erupted from the "Black Volcano" and flowed down across a broad front over the cliffs and into the sea, burying one of Tenerife's main ports. But something new emerged: the hot lava cooled in the waters of the Atlantic, where it conveniently formed *Isla Baja*, or "low island" and the locals defiantly rebuilt their new town on the only recently cooled lava.

A stroll through the old town, which still has some lovely buildings that

THE NORTHWEST & TEIDE NATIONAL PARK

Don't miss the Plaza de Pila on your walk around Icod de los Vinos

miraculously survived the eruptions, is like being in an open-air museum.

SIGHTSEEING

CASTILLO DE SAN MIGUEL
Inconceivable, but true: this tiny castle once protected Garachico from pirate attacks. The portal, adorned with coats of arms, was built in 1575. Enter through it and imagine being on the "upper deck" of the fortification and waiting for an enemy armada ... *Daily 10am–6pm | admission 2 euros | Av. Tomé Cano | 15 mins*

CONVENTO DE SAN FRANCISCO
Here too you'll find yourself transported back in time, to the year 1524. In this Franciscan monastery, you can walk as the monks once did through romantic cloisters and enter rooms with delicate stone flooring and stunning Mudéjar ceilings. Alongside the relics, you'll find a relief model of Tenerife marking the locations of lava flows in recent centuries. There are also multimedia installations showing all the Earth's hotspots of volcanic activity. Next door, the *Casa de la Cultura* has temporary art exhibitions. *Mon–Fri 10am–7pm, Sat, Sun 10am–3pm | admission 2 euros | Plaza de la Libertad*

GARACHICO

El Caletón, Garachico's natural swimming pool

EL CALETÓN NATURAL SWIMMING POOLS

Need a cool down after your walk? The streams of lava that cooled down in the sea are not only picturesque; they have also created natural bathing pools. When the sea is calm (but only then!), you can use the steps and metal ladders to climb down from the rocks into the sea for a swim.

IGLESIA DE SANTA ANA

The main church (1520) is just three steps away from the convent. Here too, you'll find wooden Mudéjar ceilings and lava-stone pillars in the dimly lit space. The sorrowful and suffering saints at the main altar were carved by Luján Pérez, the Canaries' star sculptor in the 18th century. And take a look at the clock, which has been ticking with Swiss precision since time immemorial! *Mon–Sat 10am–5pm | admission 2 euros*

EATING & DRINKING

EL REBOJO

Expect the unexpected in this unfussy, elegant restaurant: tomatoes filled with confit of tuna, perhaps; parrot fish baked in banana leaves, or cheesecake made from smoked Teno goat's cheese. Otherwise, go for the simple option and order *"dos bocados, dos vinos"* ("two tapas and two wines"). *Fri-Tue 1–10pm | C/ Martínez de Fuentes 17 | tel. 922 83 11 98 | €€–€€€*

THE NORTHWEST & TEIDE NATIONAL PARK

CAÑADA DE GARACHICO
You'll be well looked after at Mariela and Gabriel's place, diagonally opposite the castle. Whether you sit on the streetside terrace or in the comfortable dining room, you'll be served unusual tapas and main courses: we recommend the banana and cheese tortilla and the prawn skewers. *Wed–Sun noon–10pm | Av. Tomé Cano 4 | tel. 928 83 01 17 | canadadegarachico.net | €€*

SHOPPING

ARTSHOP
Everything here is made by local artists who have found inspiration on the island. Guanche-style pottery, lava-stone jewellery, paintings and photos. *C/ Esteban Ponte 3*

AROUND GARACHICO

6 LOS SILOS
6km/5 mins west of Garachico on the TF-42

A tiered white church on a plaza with a pavilion forms the centre of the pleasantly sleepy village of Los Silos (pop. 5,500). Diagonally opposite the church in an old convent is an attractive visitor centre. The *Centro de Visitantes (Tue–Sat 8am–3pm | admission free | Plaza de la Luz 10)* provides helpful information on local geology, flora and fauna, and walking opportunities in the Teno Mountains.

The road ends at a much-too-tall apartment block – an eyesore in otherwise stunning surroundings. As there are no local beaches, there's a swimming pool here where you can swim a few lengths, while looking longingly at the ocean. There is also a 15m-long skeleton of a pollock whale that got stranded here in 2005 – now it's a symbol for the conservation of sea life. *C–D4*

7 EL TANQUE
6km/12 mins southwest of Garachico on the TF-421/TF-82

The next village up from Garachico may not look like much, but it has a very unusual attraction. The *Camello Center* offers guided tours through the volcanic landscape … on camels. To make the whole thing more surreal, they dress you up in Bedouin clothing. The ride lasts just 20 minutes but afterwards you can visit the goats, ponies and donkeys in the petting zoo. There is also a restaurant offering traditional food. Be aware that if you arrive at the same time as a big tour bus, waiting times can be extremely long. *Daily 10am–5pm | admission 12 euros, children (3–10 years) 9 euros | El Tanque, TF-82, Km 10.2 | tel. 922 13 61 91 | camellocenter.es | D4*

8 BUENAVISTA DEL NORTE
11km/10 mins west of Garachico on the TF-42

The name says it all: *buena vista* ("good view") over rugged cliffs and the vast Atlantic. Tenerife's most westerly town (pop. 5,400) is tucked in beneath the impressive *Teno*

AROUND GARACHICO

The pretty village of Masca sits hidden among the Teno Mountains

Mountains. The TF-445 heads west to Buenavista Golf (green fee: 1 round 114 euros, half price in summer | tel. 922 12 90 34 | buenavistagolf.es), an 18-hole golf course in a stunning coastal location. The road carries on past the *Mirador de Don Pompeyo*, a spectacular viewpoint, before it ends at the *Punta de Teno (risk of landslide if wet and windy so the road is often closed, compulsory shuttle service on bus 369 from the church square in Buenavista)*. An old lighthouse stands alongside the new one. On clear days the view extends as far as the islands of La Palma and La Gomera. *C4*

9 MACIZO DE TENO

20km/30 mins southwest of Garachico

It's hard to believe that the Teno Mountains were once an island on their own. Seven million years ago, they rose from the sea bed and didn't become part of the "main island" around Teide until many more volcanic eruptions connected the two. Even today, the 1,000m-high Teno Mountains seem remote and inaccessible with their rugged gorges, steep cliffs and only the occasional green plateau. The *Mirador de Cherfe*, on the road from Santiago del Teide to Masca, offers a great view of the world from the top of the rugged rocks.

THE NORTHWEST & TEIDE NATIONAL PARK

If you love this wild, unspoilt terrain, keep going and then, just south of El Palmar, turn to the west towards Teno Alto (*III B6*). You pass a picnic spot and, after about 3km, you will reach this remote hamlet spread across a windswept upland plateau. Grazing on the pastures are goats and sheep, whose milk is used to make award-winning cheese. Try this delicacy with a glass of wine in one of the bars on the church square. *III C4*

10 MASCA ★

25km/50 mins southwest of Garachico on the TF-42/TF-436

Even as you approach along the narrow, bendy road, you will barely catch a glimpse of this beautiful village in the middle of the Teno Mountains. The houses, spread across the hillside, were built with blocks of stone hewn from the grey-brown rock found in the surrounding area. Until well into the 20th century, ancient shepherd tracks created by the Guanches were the only link with the outside world. The best time to explore Masca is either early in the morning or later in the evening, when the place is not overrun by tourists. Below the main road you will find a number of tourist cafés, with terraces overlooking the mountains and the valleys, e.g. *Casa Fidel (Tue–Sat 10am–5pm | tel. 922 86 34 57 | €)*. If you want to hike the spectacular *Masca Gorge (caminobarrancodemasca.com)*, be sure to check ahead for any restrictions. *III C4*

11 SANTIAGO DEL TEIDE

19km/30 mins southwest of Garachico on the TF-82

On the way to the Teno Mountains you'll pass through Santiago. This is where the booming holiday resorts around Los Gigantes are managed from – a gold mine for the village. It has a population of 5,400 and is situated on a high plateau with a domed parish church. Behind the church is *La Casona del Patio (Av. de la Iglesia 72 | tel. 922 83 92 93 | lacasonadelpatio.com | €€)*, a venerable winemaking estate that dates back to the year 1663. Two huge traditional wine presses at the entrance to the restaurant make it pretty clear what they do best here.

> **INSIDER TIP**
> **Winemaking the old-fashioned way**

Are you interested in traditional handicrafts? Then the hamlet of *Arguayo* south of Santiago is just for you. It was once an important centre for Tenerife's pottery trade. Today the craft only survives at the 🐖 *Museo del Alfarero (Tue–Sat 10am–1pm and 4–7pm, Sun 10am–2pm | admission free)*. This pottery museum is housed in a renovated workshop. Following traditional Guanche methods – i.e. no potter's wheel or tools – all its ceramics are fired in an old kiln. The finished products – simple dishes and pots made from natural clay – are all on sale. The exhibits include some of the finest pieces the potters have produced and some old photographs from the days when business was booming. *III C–D 4–5*

PARQUE NACIONAL DEL TEIDE

(□ E–F 4–6) **Majestic and remote, a trip to Tenerife's national park should be a part of every itinerary. The *Parque Nacional del Teide* reaches impressive altitudes above 2,000m and covers an area of over 135km², making it the largest national park in the Canary Islands. At its heart lies a giant crater by the name of *Las Cañadas*, in the shadow of the almost 4,000m-high Mount Teide.**

The elliptical Cañadas crater, with a diameter of 16km, is one of the world's largest, with a jagged rocky rim measuring 45km. It's so big it beggars belief. This is a landscape of superlatives. Multicoloured shimmering volcanic rock, broad plains and deep gorges alongside scree slopes – sometimes smooth and polished, sometimes pock-marked. "Mustard Mountain" *(Montaña Mostaza)* shines sulphur yellow and "White Mountain" *(Montaña Blanca)* gleams bright white,

Don't miss the Roques de García on your walk through the national park

THE NORTHWEST & TEIDE NATIONAL PARK

while the rounded slag heaps are jet black. Rocks, slammed into the earth, have jagged edges like black glass. Everywhere you go, you'll be surrounded by boulders that look as if they've been strewn by giants. And above it all, the striking peaks. The 3,000m-high volcanic chimney of the *Pico Viejo* towers on the northern edge of the two craters, where the last major eruption occurred in 1798.

Recent studies suggest, however, that both the Cañadas and the Orotava Valley were formed by landslides of an almost unimaginable scale. Some 1,000m³ of earth fell into the sea during the formation of Las Cañadas. It has been established that Mount Teide was formed almost 200,000 years ago, after the landslides, and so in geological terms is still very young. To compare, it was seven million years ago that volcanic activity here raised land from the floor of the Atlantic for the first time, forming one of several islands that would later fuse to make Tenerife.

The apparent lack of vegetation in the national park may make you feel as if you're on another planet. However, this impression is deceptive as 139 species have adjusted to the extreme climatic conditions at high altitude. They have to contend with strong sunshine during the day, freezing temperatures at night and drought. A good 20 per cent of plants are endemic to Tenerife, i.e. they don't exist anywhere else in the world. These include the pillared *tajinaste rojo* with its bright red flowers (Mount Teide bugloss), the little yellow or white Teide daisy and the purple Teide violet. Plants at this altitude stay in flower for only a short period, just May and June. Few vertebrates survive in these harsh conditions, with rewilded mouflon sheep, finches and kestrels being among the exceptions.

There are two places you should definitely not miss in the Parque Nacional. First are the *Roques de García (□ F8)*, an ensemble of multi-coloured rocky outcrops (see Discovery tour 4). A viewing platform offers a spectacular view. If you climb a little higher, you will be rewarded with a stunning vista down into the *Llano de*

PARQUE NACIONAL DEL TEIDE

The huge boulders on Mount Teide are known as "Huevos del Teide" (Teide Eggs)

Ucanca, the largest plain in the Teide-Cañadas and also of *Los Azulejos*, a shimmering greenish-blue rock formation.

The second stop is the *Pico del Teide* (F8) itself, whose almost symmetrical summit reaches a height of 3,718m. Its name is derived from the Guanche word for "hell". Hot sulphur steaming out from its slopes is proof that hell still stirs.

The ● *Teleférico (daily 9am–4pm in good weather, usually closed for maintenance in May | round trip 39 euros | volcanoteide.com | book in advance to avoid queues)*, the Mount Teide cable car, climbs 1,200m to the *La Rambleta* mountain station at 3,555m in 10 minutes. From there you can walk to *La Fortaleza* lookout point and the *Pico Viejo* (3,135m). But be warned: there are often high winds!

SIGHTS IN THE NATIONAL PARK

12 CENTRO DE VISITANTES EL PORTILLO

How was El Teide formed? What forces were at work? And how does any life survive in this volcanic desert? The national park's visitor centre helps you get to grips with the park. It has an attractive garden around the building where they grow mountain plants that you may encounter in the park itself. *Daily 9am–4.15pm | admission free | TF-21, Km32.1 on the northeastern*

THE NORTHWEST & TEIDE NATIONAL PARK

exit of the Cañadas | tel. 922 35 60 00 | F5

13 OBSERVATORIO DEL TEIDE

A setting worthy of science fiction. These metallic white observatory towers at the eastern entrance stare up into the blue sky, which is so clear that you get a good view of the whole universe. When the Canarian Institute of Astrophysics started its work up here in 1964, it seemed that this spot – well away from civilisation and at an altitude of 2,390m – was the ideal place to view the heavens.

But today the lights from the holiday resorts interfere with the work of the astronomers, so they now observe the night sky from the neighbouring island of La Palma and scientists at Tenerife's Observatory study the sun during the day. **INSIDER TIP Starlight Express** On a 90-minute tour, you can learn about how the observatory works and get to look up at the universe through a telescope. Register at volcanoteide.com | from 21 euros, children free | G5

EATING & DRINKING

PARADOR NACIONAL
The chalet-style *Parador* (hotel belonging to a state-run chain) offers excellent Canarian cuisine in the restaurant or a snack in the café which has a view of El Teide. *Las Cañadas del Teide | tel. 922 38 64 15 | parador.es | €-€€€ |* F6

SPORT & ACTIVITIES

WALKING ★
Marked walking paths lead through *Las Cañadas* and up to Pico del Teide. When climbing Spain's highest mountain, you'll pass by the "Teide Eggs", *Huevos del Teide*, huge boulders of lava rock scattered about the area.

You can pick up free information leaflets from the *El Portillo* visitor centre.

SLEEP WELL IN THE NORTHWEST

PARK HIDEAWAY
"There is a palm tree for every guest" according to the motto at *Tigaiga (83 rooms and suites | Parque Taoro 28 | tel. 922 38 35 00 | tigaiga.com | €€-€€€)* in Puerto de la Cruz. The hotel sits in a green oasis surrounded by exotic plants and it has a great view of both Teide and the sea at Puerto de la Cruz. They also offer excellent botanical tours.

HISTORIC MANOR HOUSE
You can see the sea from the roof terrace of *Hotel Gara (16 rooms | C/ Esteban de Ponte 7 | tel. 922 83 11 68 | garahotel.com | €€).* You'll eat breakfast in the romantic inner courtyard and sleep under the rafters. Step outside and you'll find yourself in Garachico's beautiful old town.

THE NORTHEAST

LAUREL FORESTS & HIP CITIES

The Cumbre Dorsal mountains separate Tenerife's two coasts like a backbone, climbing towards Pico del Teide in the southwest and the largely inaccessible Montañas de Anaga in the northeast. Only two winding roads lead up into this 1,000m-high mountain range.

It's a place of unspoiled landscapes and modern urban life. The capital, Santa Cruz, has merged with the UNESCO-protected La Laguna to form the *Zona Metropolitana*, where almost half of

Montañas de Anaga

Tinerfeños live. Over the last few years, lots of money has been spent sprucing up the two cities. Now they just need a solution to their awful traffic congestion …

Away from the Zona Metropolitana, fertile valleys form Tenerife's "breadbasket" and the biggest wine region in the Canary Islands. Unfortunately, this area has not escaped the impact of mass tourism: large stretches of the coast have been overdeveloped and the valleys have been built up.

THE NORTHEAST

Punta del Hidalgo p. 83

Bajamar p. 83

Swim in natural pools as you watch spectacular sunsets from Punta del Hidalgo and Bajamar.

Tegueste

Tamarco

La Laguna and Santa Cruz comprise Tenerife's *Zona Metropolitana* and are home to 360,000 people, nearly half the island's population. There's plenty to see and do here …

7 Valle de Guerra

TF5

La Laguna ★ p. 77

Tacoronte p. 81

La Costurera

TF24

4 El Sauzal

Don't get in a mix up when you book your flight! Tenerife Norte Ciudad de la Laguna airport largely serves the other Canary Islands rather than the rest of Europe.

5 La Matanza de Acentejo

28km, 30 mins

La Esperanza

Llano del Mo

6 La Victoria de Acentejo

ESPAÑA

TF24

El Tablero

T e n e r i f e

3 Cumbre Dorsal ★

✓ 1

TF1

Arafo

MARCO POLO BUCKET LIST

1 ✓ Cruise above the clouds

Driving the TF-24 road along the island's spine will lead you to spectacular lookout points, such as the *Mirador de Ortuño*
▶ p. 80

5 ✓ Tune in

You can listen to everything from classical to pop in the *Auditorio de Tenerife*, one of the most innovative buildings in the Canary Islands ▶ p. 71

The ridge of the Anaga Mountains is covered in laurel trees. Serpentine roads descend from here to the north coast where you'll find wave-battered bays and good fish restaurants.

Culture is writ large in Santa Cruz and La Laguna (Tenerife's current and former capitals). Attend a concert, visit one of the museums or get to know some contemporary artists.

MARCO POLO HIGHLIGHTS

★ **SANTA CRUZ DE TENERIFE**
The island's capital has enchanting parks, great art and magnificent music ➤ p. 70

★ **PALMETUM**
Palm trees growing on what used to be a landfill site ➤ p. 72

★ **TENERIFE ESPACIO DE LAS ARTES**
Santa Cruz's art centre, the TEA, is sensational both inside and out ➤ p. 74

★ **PLAYA DE LAS TERESITAS**
At weekends this gem of a beach attracts thousands of *Tinerfeños* ➤ p. 76

★ **LA LAGUNA**
Travel back in time to the colonial period at this UNESCO World Heritage Site ➤ p. 77

★ **CUMBRE DORSAL**
A tour along the "backbone of Tenerife" will reveal virtually every type of flora on the island ➤ p. 80

★ **MONTAÑAS DE ANAGA**
Rugged ridges, gargantuan gorges and isolated inlets ➤ p. 84

SANTA CRUZ DE TENERIFE

SANTA CRUZ DE TENERIFE

(🕮 K2–3) ★ **Santa Cruz de Tenerife** stretches back from the coast towards the jagged mountains on a series of terraces. Plain apartment blocks and stately colonial buildings harmoniously share the space.

Although Santa Cruz (pop. 230,000) is a lively port, the pace never feels hectic. Large parts of the city have been pedestrianised; pavement bars and cafés are firmly in local hands; and Canarian laissez-faire is the order of the day.

THE NORTHEAST

The Spaniard Alonso Fernández de Lugo landed in the bay and established the first settlement here in 1494. Santa Cruz was initially overshadowed by La Laguna, 5km inland, but it has been the seat of Tenerife's government since 1723. Commercially important for the city is the sprawling port, where goods from all over the world are traded and where thousands of cruise ship passengers disembark each year.

WHERE TO START

The **bus station (Estación Central de Guaguas)** is just south of the city centre. On your way to the old town from here, you will pass the market *(mercado)* and the TEA arts centre. If you are coming by car, try and find a space as close to the **Plaza de España** as possible, and set off to explore from there.

SIGHTSEEING

AUDITORIO DE TENERIFE ✓

The snow-white concert hall is a daring building designed by Spain's star architect, Santiago Calatrava. Its most striking feature is the trio of huge, shell-shaped wings arching over the auditorium, giving the building an airborne, almost weightless appearance. However, it is not only visually impressive as the acoustics are also extraordinarily good. Every week, concerts in all musical genres – from world music to classical – as well as opera and ballet performances are held in the bright and airy auditorium. There is a shop and café, and architectural tours of the building are available *(Mon–Fri 10am–5pm, Sat 10am–2pm | book at the ticket desk, or tel. 922 56 86 25 or email visitas@auditoriodetenerife.com). Av. de la Constitución | auditoriodetenerife.com*

INSIDER TIP Music for everyone

CASA DEL CARNAVAL 👹

Missed the carnival? No problem! Here, you can slip into a crazy costume before admiring those of queens and drag queens alike. There are also plenty of 3D videos of carnival in full swing. *Daily 10am–6pm | admission free | C/ Aguere 15 | casacarnavalsantacruz.com | ⏱ 30 mins*

CENTRO CULTURAL EL TANQUE 🐖

This place is somewhat out of the way, but it's worth the detour: a gigantic oil tank has been transformed into an art centre by top architect Fernando Menis. The subdued light in the tank imbues the installations and sculptures with a particular magic. Concerts are sometimes held here in the evening. The "Keroxen" rock events *(keroxen.com)* are legendary and take their name from the kerosene that was once stored here. *Tue–Fri 11am–2pm and 5–8pm, Sat 11am–2pm | admission free | C/ Adán Martín Menis s/n*

IGLESIA DE NUESTRA SEÑORA DE LA CONCEPCIÓN

The slender steeple of the city's oldest church (1502) was built in typical colonial style and for many years served as

SANTA CRUZ DE TENERIFE

an important landmark for sailors. Slim volcanic stone columns support the building internally. Precious Baroque works of art include a high altar, a coloured marble pulpit, paintings, gold and silver treasures and the *Holy Cross of the Conquest* dating from 1494. *Av. Bravo Murillo*

IGLESIA DE SAN FRANCISCO/ MUSEO DE BELLAS ARTES 🐷

The Franciscan monks have long since left Santa Cruz and their monastery has been turned into a gallery with works by Dutch and Spanish artists alongside a huge collection of Canarian masters. However, the church still has a religious function. Explore the sacred interior with its volcanic pillars, Baroque altars and carved wood ceilings. *Church: Plaza San Francisco | Museum: Tue–Fri 10am–8pm, Sat/Sun 10am–3pm | admission free | C/ José Murphy 12*

LA RAMBLA

This long boulevard arcs around the centre of the city. Kiosks and benches shaded by tall trees line the pedestrian walkway, inviting you to linger. Modern sculptures — including ones by Henry Moore and Joan Miró — mix high art into people's daily grind. The old bullring halfway round is now only used for sporting events and pop concerts.

MUSEO DE LA NATURALEZA Y EL HOMBRE

You'll be able to trace the island's history in this magnificent neoclassical former hospital. It starts with Tenerife's volcanic formation and the first plants that established themselves on the barren lava. Next you meet the first settlers, the Guanches, whose preserved skulls are neatly lined up in glass cases. Tools, ornaments and everyday objects belonging to the early Canarian population complete the picture. *Mon–Sat 9am–7pm, Sun 10am–5pm | admission 5 euros | C/ Fuente Morales | museosdetenerife. org |* ⏱ *1 hr*

PALMETUM ⭐

A 111-hectare botanical garden has been created where thousands of tonnes of rubbish once quietly rotted away. It contains palm trees from all over the world. Labyrinthine paths will lead you over little hills, past ponds and waterfalls. Sensitive tropical plants grow in a greenhouse to prepare them for life in the wild. *Daily 10am–6pm, last entry 5pm | admission 6 euros | Av. de la Constitución | palmetumtenerife.es |* ⏱ *1 hr*

PARQUE GARCÍA SANABRIA

Stroll down wide paths, past enormous trees and exotic flowers. Here and there, you'll run into sculptures, arcades and fountains, with enchanting squares where you can sit and catch your breath. You can also get some refreshment at the popular *cafetería* by the (lower) entrance to the park.

PLAZA DE ESPAÑA & PLAZA DE LA CANDELARIA

The broad *Plaza de España* with its gigantic circular pool of water, numerous trees and floating tropical lamps is

THE NORTHEAST

very attractive. Its fountain shoots a jet of water skywards every hour. Behind the square, two unassuming pavilions overgrown with plants are home to the tourist information centre and a crafts shop run by *Artenerife*.

The seat of the island's government administration, *Cabildo Insular*, towers over the other side of the square; an electric nativity scene erected here every year in December attracts many visitors. Near the Cabildo stands the massive memorial to the soldiers who died during the Civil War. Giant athletic warriors carrying swords and helmets – in typical fascist style – commemorate those who fought and died for the dictator Franco.

You can get away from the chilling sight by (literally) sinking into the ground. Through an unobtrusive entrance, you can descend into the underground foundations of the *Castillo de San Cristóbal (Mon–Sat 10am–6pm | admission free)*. The fortress was erected in 1575 to fend off pirates and in 1928 – unused for many years – was razed to make room for the expanding city. In the twilight you can see displays on all the city's fortifications. There's even a replica of the famous *El Tigre* cannon, which routed Admiral Nelson in 1797 and now commemorates the military history of the island.

Further inland lies the adjacent *Plaza de la Candelaria*. The "bearer of light" floats on top of a tall, white Carrara marble column – the Virgen de la Candelaria is Tenerife's patron saint. Santa Cruz's shopping district begins at Plaza de la Candelaria, with an eclectic mixture of trendy and traditional shops.

The reading room in Tenerife's Espacio de las Artes is bright and airy

PLAZA DEL PRÍNCIPE ASTURIAS

A magnificent square named after the son of the Spanish king. Mature trees and lush vegetation create the impression of a tropical oasis. Look out for the large, bronze fish statue, *El Chicharro* (The Mackerel). It is a reminder that *Tinerfeños* are often called *chicharreros*.

INSIDER TIP: Fishy nickname

SANTA CRUZ DE TENERIFE

TENERIFE ESPACIO DE LAS ARTES ★

Tenerife's ambitious art and cultural Centre (TEA) is a long building that fits snugly into the *barranco*, the long ravine running through the city towards the coast. Inside, its strictly angled lines, tall glass façades and an open patio allow plenty of light in. A permanent exhibition displays the life's work of the great Tenerife-born surrealist artist Óscar Domínguez. Alongside it are temporary exhibitions of international contemporary art. There is also a large library and a nice cafeteria. *Thu–Sun 10am–8pm | admission free | Av. de San Sebastián 10 | teatenerife.es |* ⏱ *1 hr*

EATING & DRINKING

BODEGÓN EL PUNTERO

A rustically themed restaurant with all the Canarian classics. The fish here is especially good. *Tue–Sat noon–4.30pm, 8–11pm | C/ San Clemente 3 | tel. 922 28 22 14 | €*

GUANNABÍ

A good spot in the Noria nightlife district. Stone walls with ferns growing down from the ceiling and a mish-mash of furniture make for a relaxed vibe. The food (served on cool plates) is delicious. *Daily from 1pm | C/ Antonio Domínguez Alfonso 34 | tel. 922 87 53 75 | FB: Guannabi restaurante | €€*

IL GELATO DEL MERCATO

Tenerife's best ice cream can be found in the hustle-and-bustle of the market hall. *Tue–Sun 9.30am–3pm | Av. San Sebastián 51 | Mercado de Nuestra Señora de África | €*

LA HIERBITA

The "little herb" serves local classics in the atmospheric surroundings of a historic building in the old town. Do as the Spaniards do and order lots of tapas to share. *Daily from noon | C/ Clavel 19 | tel. 922 24 46 17 | lahierbita.com | €–€€*

LOS MENCEYES

Beautifully set tables and high ceilings create an elegance to match the modern Canarian cuisine here, while an army of waiters offer excellent, unobtrusive service. Fine fusion cuisine is offered by the adjoining *Kon-Tiki (daily from noon)*, while next door *Papa Negra (Fri–Tue from 7.30pm)* provides an informal alternative. *Daily | C/ Dr Naveiras 38 | tel. 922 27 67 00 | €€€*

SHOPPING

ARTENERIFE

A low, arching pavilion covered in greenery on the Plaza de España is home to the state-run art and craft chain. *Mon–Fri 10am–2pm and 5–8pm, Sat 10am–2pm | artenerife.com*

EL CORTE INGLÉS

A large department store offering everything from the clothes to fine foods. On the seventh floor there is a panoramic restaurant *(€)*. *Av. Tres de Mayo*

THE NORTHEAST

Nuestra Señora de África market is loved by locals and tourists alike

MERCADO DE NUESTRA SEÑORA DE ÁFRICA

Exploring Santa Cruz's Moorish-style town market is an exhilarating experience. On Sundays there's also a flea market. *Daily 7am–3pm | C/ San Sebastián 51*

SPORT & ACTIVITIES

PARQUE MARÍTIMO CÉSAR MANRIQUE

This water park has lots of pools, islands of volcanic rock and plenty of space for sunbathing and makes for a great day out. It was designed by the artist César Manrique. Small cafés serve drinks and snacks. *Daily 10am–6pm | admission 5 euros, children 1.50 euros | Av. de la Constitución 5*

NIGHTLIFE

At the weekend, clubbers converge on *La Noria* area at the edge of the *Barranco* (between the church and the bridge) and then party until the small hours.

LA NORIA NIGHTLIFE AREA

An atmospherically lit network of pedestrian-only streets lined with bars and bodegas. Start your night with a relaxed drink at *Bulan*. After that take your pick from the densely packed bars: in *Lagar* there's live music; opposite is the Mexican restaurant *El Rincón de Guadalupe* (elrincondeguadalupe.com) and then the cosy Andalusian *Tasca El Porrón*. *All daily from 8pm | C/ Antonio Domínguez Alfonso*

AROUND SANTA CRUZ DE TENERIFE

FESTIVALS

Santa Cruz's biggest festival is *Carnaval*, which is celebrated to great excess over several weeks (see p. 20). Many also travel specifically to the *Festival de Música de Canarias (festival decanarias.com)*, which features a top-class line up in the spectacular *Auditorio* (see p. 71)

AROUND SANTA CRUZ DE TENERIFE

🟧 SAN ANDRÉS
10km/10 mins northeast of Santa Cruz on the TF-11

When Santa Cruz's city authorities decided they needed a beach, they headed to this fishing village. However, the volcanic pebbles were not attractive enough, so in 1970 they brought in a few shiploads of fine Saharan sand from what was then the Spanish colony of Western Sahara and thus transformed the village into a resort.

Gleaming brightly in golden yellow, the man-made 1km-long ★ 🌴 *Playa de las Teresitas* is now much enhanced by clusters of palm trees. Breakwaters were created to prevent the golden sands from being washed away. During the week it is often quiet. But at the weekend Cruzeños flock here in their thousands. Nevertheless, this most Canarian of beaches is still something of a hidden gem among tourists.

The sea breeze whets the appetite, so try out one of the beach bars or the restaurants that line the main road. Their produce comes (mostly) fresh from the boats that head out to sea from here. *La Estrella del Mar (Wed–Mon 1–10pm | C/ Dique 22 | €€)* and *Marisquería Ramón (Wed–Mon noon–9pm | C/ El Dique 23 | €€)* have good reputations, large dining rooms and live fish and lobster tanks. 📖 *K–L2*

🟧 GRAN CANARIA
73km/80 mins east of Santa Cruz (on the ferry)

For a day trip to the neighbouring island to the east (for everything you need to know, see MARCO POLO *Gran*

THE NORTHEAST

Canaria) take the Fred Olsen Express catamaran from the harbour. This runs several times a day to Agaete and the crossing takes an hour *(return trip from 100 euros/pers. | tel. 902 10 01 07 | fredolsen.es)*. 0

LA LAGUNA

(*J2*) **Do you want to stroll through historic streets, visit ancient monasteries and eat in a rustic bodega? ★ La Laguna, a UNESCO World Heritage Site, is great for a day trip – or a longer stay.**

But few people want to spend their entire holiday here, because up on the plateau it can get cool and cloudy – at an altitude of 500m, the town is often right in the middle of trade-wind clouds. What is now a nightmare for holidaymakers was once a blessing for settlers. The cool, moist air ensured bountiful harvests, first for the Guanches, then for the Spanish conquerors. It's not surprising that they made La Laguna the island's first capital in 1496.

It wasn't long before the town had become the archipelago's intellectual centre too. In 1701 the first university in the Canary Islands was founded here. Although in 1723 it lost political

Sunbathe among the palms and swim in the calm water at Playa de las Teresitas

LA LAGUNA

power to the emerging town of Santa Cruz, with its university and an episcopal seat, La Laguna remains the cultural heart of Tenerife and it continues to be a vibrant city of 156,000 inhabitants. Its colonial legacy is still evident and nurtured, as is reflected in the many fine, typically Canarian buildings.

SIGHTSEEING

IGLESIA DE NUESTRA SEÑORA DE LA CONCEPCIÓN

La Laguna's oldest church (1496) has a beautiful painted wooden ceiling, a magnificently carved Baroque pulpit and a baptismal font brought over by the Spanish conqueror Alonso Fernández de Lugo. From the tall bell tower next to the church you can enjoy a fantastic view of the town and the highlands. *Mon 10am–2pm, Tue–Fri 10am–5pm | C/ Obispo Rey Redondo*

LA CATEDRAL DE LOS REMEDIOS

Tenerife's cathedral was built in the 20th century on the ruins of an older church from 1511. Many works of art are preserved from the original building, including expressive sculptures by the Canarian artist José Luján Pérez. The concrete dome completed in 2014 has added a new sense of space and light. *Mon–Fri 9am–6pm, Sat 9.30am–12.30pm, 2–5pm | admission 7 euros incl. audio guide | Plaza Fray Albino | lalagunacatedral.com*

MUSEO DE HISTORIA DE TENERIFE

Even if you're not interested in Canarian history, this palace dating from 1593 is worth a visit. The *Casa de Lercaro (Mon–Sat 9am–7pm, Sun 10am–5pm | admission 5 euros | C/ San Agustín 22 | museosdetenerife.com)* is a superb example of colonial architecture with its courtyard's finely carved wooden galleries. In the *Fundación Cristino de Vera (admission free)* a few doors further on you can admire nearly 100 paintings by the Tenerife-born painter.

> **INSIDER TIP — Art to make you think**
> De Vera's pointillistic still lifes are slightly morbid – perfect for a holiday meditation on the transience of human life!

MUSEO DE LA CIENCIA Y EL COSMOS

You will spot the Museum of Science and the Cosmos with its planetarium long before you get there, thanks to its huge radio telescope. At over 70 different playful and interactive "stations", you can learn about the connections between the Earth, Sun, Solar System and Milky Way and about human

---

WHERE TO START

Whether you arrive by car, bus or tram, your first stop really ought to be the city's historic centre. The best place to start an exploratory tour of the city is the **Plaza del Adelantado**. This is near the *tourist information office (C/ Obispo Rey Redondo 7 | tel. 922 63 11 94 | turismodelalaguna.com)* where you can book free guided tours of the city.

THE NORTHEAST

existence in a way that will entertain adults and children alike. *Mon–Sat 9am–7pm, Sun 10am–5pm | admission 5 euros, children under 8 years free | Av. Los Menceyes 70 | museosdetenerife.com | ⏱ 2 hrs*

EATING & DRINKING

BODEGÓN TUCOYO
This place has been serving Spanish tapas in simple, rustic surroundings for generations. There's also house wine (produced on the premises and served in empty Fanta bottles!) or local Dorada beer. Before your meal, you'll be given a bowl of monkey nuts – it's customary to drop the shells onto the floor … *Mon–Sat noon–3pm, 7pm–2am | C/ Juan de Vera 16 | tel. 922 25 00 45 | €*

LA BOURMET
The name is a combination of "burger" and "gourmet". They offer more than ten different burgers, sweet potato fries and home-made bread served with local beers and wines. *Daily noon–10.30pm | C/ Herradores 46 | tel. 922 25 04 13 | labourmet.com | €*

LAGUNA NIVARIA

> **INSIDER TIP**
> **Scintillating snacks and fine dining**

The charming bistro in the hotel of the same name is a popular spot for *Tinerfeños*. If you want something a bit fancier, where the finest organic ingredients are transformed into creative Canarian dishes, head to the main restaurant instead. *Mon–Thu 1–4pm and 7–10.30pm | C/ del Consistorio 13/ Plaza del Adelantado 11 | tel. 922 26 42 98 | lagunanivaria.com | €€*

The huge radio telescope at the Museo de la Ciencia y el Cosmos

SHOPPING

In the pedestrian-priority streets you'll find old-fashioned corner shops as well as trendy boutiques. For a culinary hit, visit the overflowing stalls of the *market hall (daily 7am–2pm | Plaza del Cristo)* – where you can pick up a coffee and a ham sandwich. For eye-catching footwear, head to

AROUND LA LAGUNA

Pisaverde (C/ Juan de Vera | pisaverde store.com); the cheeky designs for him and her are made from banana fibres – after all, *"pisa verde"* means something like "green step". (but can also refer to a snappy dresser). There are also matching accessories, such as wallets, bags and belts.

INSIDER TIP Banana shoes

NIGHTLIFE

La Laguna is where the island's young people come to party. In *C/ Herradores* and *C/ Obispo Rey Redondo*, one bodega follows the next and there are also lots of bars to the south of *Plaza del Adelantado* towards the university district.

AROUND LA LAGUNA

3 CUMBRE DORSAL ★

10km/10 mins southwest of La Laguna (if driving take the TF-24)
The 42km road following the narrow mountain ridge from La Laguna to Teide National Park is the most scenic drive on Tenerife. Passing through a kaleidoscope of varied landscapes, the road climbs to a height of 2,300m. To the west of the old capital, cacti and orange trees bask on the arid plateau, at the centre of which is *La Esperanza*, a neat, if rather sleepy, village. *Esperanza Forest* begins higher up. Dense forests and tall eucalyptus trees keep the soil cool, ferns find shade, and laurel and pine plantations will hopefully make up for centuries of deforestation. The rustic *Las Lagunetas* restaurant *(closed Mon | €)* in the heart of the forest not only serves great food – its setting is like something out of a story book, especially in the fog.

INSIDER TIP Fairytale pit-stop

From the *Mirador Montaña Grande*, at 1,120m, you can see La Palma on one side, and Gran Canaria on the other. However, your clear views may quickly be enveloped in cloud. Also visible from the ● *Mirador de Ortuño* is the (sometimes snow-capped) peak of Pico del Teide. In summer seven red watchtowers, one of which is visible on the left, are manned around the clock as forest fires are the biggest threat to this region.

At 2,000m the road reaches the tree line. The rocks are craggy and only pines, gorse bushes and low shrubs can stand the often-harsh winds and wide temperature fluctuations. Jagged ridges of volcanic rock along with black, leaden and red fields of ash, are evidence of volcanic eruptions that took place millions of years ago (the last one was over 100 years ago). Just past the white towers of the *Observatory*, you will reach the *Centro de Visitantes El Portillo* (see p. 64), the national park's visitor centre and the start of the lunar landscape surrounding Pico del Teide. *G–J 2–4*

THE NORTHEAST

The Cumbre Dorsal has amazing views of the Pico del Teide

TACORONTE

(□ H2) **As so often on Tenerife, a ring of bland new buildings surrounds the town but in the middle lurks a pretty historical centre.**

For wine connoisseurs, it is definitely worth a visit, because Tacoronte (pop. 22,000) lies at the heart of the largest wine-growing area on the Canary Islands. Extensive vineyards extend along the fertile hillsides. The dozens of *bodegas* will try and tempt you into stopping for a glass. Look out for signs saying "Guachinche". These are basic bars serving young wine alongside good-value, hearty dishes.

INSIDER TIP
Gourmet pit-stop

SIGHTSEEING

EL CRISTO DE LOS DOLORES

This life-sized statue of Jesus dating from the 17th century stands in the church of a former Augustinian monastery. The triple-naved church contains a wealth of sacred silverwork and its monastery (now a cultural centre) has a lovely cloister. *Daily | Plaza del Cristo*

AROUND TACORONTE

4 EL SAUZAL

3km/5 mins southwest of Tacoronte on the TF-215

Most visitors to Tacoronte's neighbouring town (pop. 8,000) head for the

AROUND TACORONTE

Casa del Vino (Tue–Sat 10am–8pm, Sun 10am–6pm | admission free, wine tastings bookable online from 12 euros for 3 wines, incl. cheese | tel. 922 57 25 35 | casadelvinotenerife.com). The "House of Wine" is located in a 17th-century farmhouse with a lovely view of the sea and of Mount Teide. You'll see historic equipment including wooden presses and much more, documenting the history of wine production on Tenerife.

In the Honey House and the "Agro-Diversity Visitor Centre" you can learn about all the island's edible products. A walk through the vineyards is also fun. If you have a car, you can drive 1.5km down to the town centre which "hangs" over the coastal cliffs on several terraces. Behind the ornate 16th-century Iglesia de San Pedro, you'll discover a romantic spot with a *museum (irregular opening hours)* dedicated to Tenerife's unofficial patron saint, Sor María de Jesús. Also lovely is the *Mirador de Garañona* with its view of the surf thundering against the cliffs. *H2*

5 LA MATANZA DE ACENTEJO

5km/7 mins southwest of Tacoronte on the TF-215

A town whose name means the "slaughter of Acentejo" and recalls the momentous battle of 1494 between the Guanches and the Spanish. On that occasion, the conquistadors suffered a humiliating defeat. Unfortunately, there's hardly anything old left in La Matanza. The exception is *Casa Juan (Wed–Sun 1–10pm | C/ Acentejo 77 | tel. 922 57 70 12 | casajuan.net | €€).* Delicious Mediterranean and central European cuisine has been served in a contemporary rustic setting for two generations. Try the home-smoked fish! *H3*

INSIDER TIP
Smoking!

6 LA VICTORIA DE ACENTEJO

9km/10 mins southwest of Tacoronte on the TF-215/TF-217

That the Spanish eventually subjugated the Guanches is recalled 2km further on in the name of La Matanza's neighbouring village: La Victoria de Acentejo. Just over a year after the defeat, the Spaniards returned, but this time with shining armour and an even larger army. The Guanches now had nothing with which to counter them and were finally defeated. To give thanks to God, Captain Fernández de Lugo ordered his men to start work on a church, which was fittingly named *Nuestra Señora de las Victorias*. It stands to this day. *G–H3*

7 VALLE DE GUERRA

9km/10 mins northeast of Tacoronte on the TF-16

The Valle de Guerra region north of Tacoronte is an important area for wine and fruit and vegetable growing. On the left, just before you enter the town of the same name, is a grand house which holds the *Museo de Antropología de Tenerife (daily 10am–5pm | admission 5 euros | museosdetenerife.com).* It's a rather pompous name for a decent museum on everyday life through the ages. *H2*

THE NORTHEAST

The Casa del Vino is a wine museum with tasting rooms, tapas bar and restaurant

BAJAMAR & PUNTA DEL HIDALGO

(*J1*) **Bajamar and Punta del Hidalgo are among the quieter resorts on the island and they are currently undergoing a facelift to make amends for much of the 1960s development.**

Bajamar boasts a promenade and two large, free, 🐷 *natural swimming pools (Piscinas Naturales)*, which use seawater direct from the ocean. Even if the sea is crashing into the pool's walls, you can carry on calmly swimming your lengths.

INSIDER TIP
Swim safe from the surf

There is also a natural swimming pool in *Punta del Hidalgo*. From there, you can walk about 4km along the coast, past the lighthouse to the "Rock of the Two Brothers" (see p. 84) – two cliffs at the base of the Anaga range. Both Bajamar and Punta del Hidalgo offer great places to stay for those not interested in package tours, etc.

EATING & DRINKING

COFRADÍA DE PESCADORES PUNTA HIDALGO
Go for a swim in the natural pool at *Punta del Hidalgo*, then enjoy some fish in this restaurant run by the fishermen's association – preferably at sunset. *Daily noon–11pm | C/ Hoya Baja/Av. Marítima 46, Punta del Hidalgo | tel. 922 15 69 54 | €–€€*

AROUND BAJAMAR & PUNTA DEL HIDALGO

The village of Taganana on the edge of the Anaga Mountains

AROUND BAJAMAR & PUNTA DEL HIDALGO

8 CHINAMADA

9km/3½ hrs east of Punta del Hidalgo (follow the marked paths on foot PR-TF 10)

TF-13 coastal road peters out in Punta del Hidalgo. At the end there's an impressive view over the north coast and the *Roque de los Dos Hermanos*, ("Rock of the Two Brothers"). Starting below the bend is a marked hiking trail to *Chinamada*, dramatically situated among the cliffs. Its residents live (as they have for centuries) in whitewashed dwellings carved out of the tufa rock. *J1*

MONTAÑAS DE ANAGA

(*J-L 1–2*) **Northeast of Santa Cruz and La Laguna, increasingly windy roads climb up into the cool ★ Anaga Mountains. For millions of years a laurel forest has survived in this remote area, where there is still very little human habitation.**

These steep inclines were out of reach even for the Spanish settlers, who from the outset indiscriminately felled the island's forests. In many places the woodland is interspersed with gnarled laurel trees, from whose branches hang metre-long strands of lichen that resemble old men's beards. Like sponges they absorb moisture from the trade-wind clouds, which ascend in dense swathes. If the mist clears, the *miradores* (viewing points)

THE NORTHEAST

style altarpiece in *Nuestra Señora de las Nieves*, a church built in 1506. Down on the coast, the fishermen's hamlets of *Roque de las Bodegas* and *Benijo* face the wrath of the waves. If you stay up at the top, you will get to *Mirador El Bailadero*, which has a stunning view of the steep cliffs on this stretch of coast.

afford fantastic long-distance views. The sweeping panorama from the highest, *Pico del Inglés* (992m), takes in the Atlantic surf at Punta del Hidalgo and the beach at Las Teresitas. At the Mirador Cruz del Carmen, marked footpaths wind through rugged mountain terrain. The *visitor centre (daily 9.30am–4pm)* has leaflets detailing the footpaths. Try the Camino de los Sentidos, a picturesque one-hour circular walk through the "enchanted forest". You can regain your strength with dishes made using regional ingredients at *La Gangochera (daily 9am–4.30pm | tel. 922 26 42 12 | FB | €)* opposite the visitor centre.

The biggest village in these mountains is *Taganana (K1)* which sits at the foot of a broad valley under high peaks. There is a stunning Flemish-

> **INSIDER TIP**
> A walk to awaken the senses

SLEEP WELL IN THE NORTHEAST

OLD TOWN CLASSIC
Hotel Aguere (23 rooms | C/ Obispo Rey Redondo 55 | La Laguna | tel. 922 31 40 36 | hotelaguere.es | €€) has been welcoming vistors into La Laguna's old town since 1855.

A DREAM LOCATION BY THE SEA
Jardín de la Paz (11 apartments | C/ Acentejo | La Matanza | tel. 922 57 83 19 | jardinde-la-paz.com | €€€) perches on a green cliff high above the Atlantic. The view is breathtaking, and so is the breakfast, which is served in either the greenhouse or the garden, surrounded by exotic plants. What about the studios and suites? Well, they're the height of luxury and comfort.

THE SOUTHEAST

SEMI-DESERT BETWEEN MOUNTAINS & COAST

There are few hidden charms in this region. Arid land, over-developed resorts and a handful of sleepy towns. And it can get very dusty – and gusty – with trade winds casting a veil over the sun. There are some gems here, though, like Candelaria, a place of pilgrimage on the coast, and El Médano, whose natural beaches are the island's biggest.

Once you get a bit higher, it gets prettier. There are endless lines of pumice stone walls criss-crossing between terraced fields where fruit

The Basílica is home to the Virgen de Candelaria

and vegetables are grown. Lots of wine is produced here and the pastures are home to goats and sheep whose milk is used to make excellent cheese.

The drive along winding TF-28 highway from Los Cristianos to Santa Cruz de Tenerife is worthwhile. There are many fine views en route and traditional villages where little has changed even with the arrival of mass tourism.

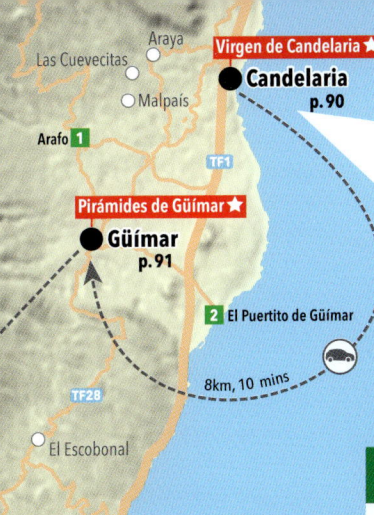

Candelaria is Tenerife's patron saint, so it's no surprise that nearly everything in this pilgrimage town serves the "light-bearing Madonna".

MARCO POLO BUCKET LIST

7 ✓ **Beachside entertainment**
Wind- and kitesurfers put on a show for the beach-goers at *Playa El Médano* ➤ p.94

Consistent wind plus a long, undeveloped beach draw wind- and kitesurfers to the coast here.

MARCO POLO HIGHLIGHTS

★ **VIRGEN DE CANDELARIA**
The holiest of holies on the Canary Islands: Tenerife's Madonna ➤ p.90

★ **PIRÁMIDES DE GÜÍMAR**
Mysterious stone pyramids and a ship made of reeds ➤ p.91

★ **EL MÉDANO**
A mecca for windsurfing and popular with a younger crowd ➤ p.93

★ **PAISAJE LUNAR**
A "lunar landscape" made from volcanic rock ➤ p.97

OCÉANO
ATLÁNTICO

CANDELARIA

(*J4*) **In this small town of 20,000 inhabitants, everything revolves around the *Virgen de Candelaria*, Tenerife's patron saint.**

A huge pilgrimage is celebrated in her honour every August, and a steady stream of pilgrims arrives here all year round. Take a stroll through the old town with its occasionally steep lanes, small shops and the broad square that opens up towards the ocean.

SIGHTSEEING

BASÍLICA DE CANDELARIA

The triple-naved basilica built in 1959 in a slightly exaggerated Canarian neo-colonial style is home to the archipelago's most revered shrine, the ★ *Virgen de Candelaria*. The extravagantly clad Virgin, adorned with crown and jewels, occupies the place of honour in a gold-framed, illuminated chamber above the altar. A modern mural tells the story behind the statue. Guanche shepherds found a statue of the Virgin Mary, which they immediately declared their "magical mother". She repaid their faith by performing miracles (which continue to this day). Today's Madonna was made in 1827 by local artist, Fernando Estévez, after the original was lost during a storm.

PLAZA DE LA PATRONA DE CANARIAS

The vast square in front of the cathedral was built for the throngs of pilgrims who come every year in mid-August to pay homage to the Virgen de Candelaria. Nine rather strange, oversized *bronze statues* sit prominently on the waterfront. They were created in 1993 by Canarian artist, José Abad, and depict the *menceys*, who ruled over Tenerife at the time of the Spanish conquest. The Guanche kings are dressed in animal skins and hold spears, sticks and mallets. With their clean-shaven faces, athletic bodies and flowing hair, they embody the ideal of the "noble savage".

Beyond the statues there is a dark sandy beach which stretches 800m to the north. If you follow the promenade to the south, you will get to the impressive *Cueva de San Blas*, which is 14m long and over 5m high. This is where the shepherds are said to have found the statue of the Virgin Mary in the 14th century, and so the chapel was built on the site. However, recent archaeology has shown the caves here have served ritual purposes for at least 2,000 years.

Hungry? Head back to the Plaza de La Patrona, where *Plaza (daily 12.30–6pm | tel. 922 50 41 31 | €€)* serves homely Canarian cuisine with a sea view. After a good lunch, you may feel up to tackling the town's steep roads. The small steeple which protrudes out of the jumble of houses is the Baroque *Iglesia de Santa Ana* (1575).

SHOPPING

MERCADILLO

On Wednesdays and Saturdays, a small *market* is held at the entrance to the road leading to the Plaza de la

THE SOUTHEAST

Patrona de Canarias where farmers from the surrounding area sell fruit, vegetables, cheese and wine.

On Saturdays you will find crafts, knick-knacks and religious objects on sale at the *Centro Comercial Punta Larga*.

GÜIMAR

(□ H4) **Many people have heard of the Pyramids of Güimar, but few know the town (pop. 19,000) itself. The small old town with its churches and large houses is testament to its one-time wealth. Vineyards in the surrounding Valle de Güimar provide much-needed greenery in this dry region.**

SIGHTSEEING

IGLESIA SAN PEDRO APÓSTOL
The church, built in 1610, boasts wooden ceilings, a carved pulpit and grand circular altarpieces. The trompe l'oeil painting behind the altar appears to lengthen the nave. *Plaza San Pedro*

PIRÁMIDES DE GÜIMAR ★ ⚑
Spread over a large expanse of land to the north of the town are six stone pyramids. In the past, farmers dried their fruit and vegetables on the steps here and did not even think about the strange architecture. Why should they? The eastern part of the island was criss-crossed by stone walls and every generation added new ones. It needed an outsider to take a closer

These statues in Candelaria commemorate the old rulers of Tenerife

GÜÍMAR

The mysterious pyramids at Güímar were built out of lava stone

look at these "piles of stones" to discover their symmetrical beauty. Having studied the alignment of the pyramids and carried out a survey of their exact location, the Norwegian anthropologist Thor Heyerdahl concluded that they were probably used for sacred rituals and for astronomic observation. He also believed they formed a transatlantic link between ancient Egyptian pyramids and those of the Maya in Central America.

An *ethnographic park (daily 10am–6pm | admission 18 euros | C/ Chacona | piramidesdeguimar.es)* excellently explains these theories and casts new light on life for the Canary Islands' first settlers. Heyerdahl's work is covered in one section of the park which contains a life-size recreation of the *Ra II*, the 12m-long ship, built entirely of reeds, on which he crossed the Atlantic from Morocco to Barbados in 1970.

The *Tropicarium* is also well worth visiting. Carnivorous and poisonous plants are allowed to thrive in this small garden. Did you know that oleander plants and birds of paradise flowers are toxic?

EATING & DRINKING

CASONA SANTO DOMINGO
This town house dates from the 16th century and serves traditional food alongside good Canarian wines. *C/ Santo Domingo 32 | tel. 652 80 30 95 | casonasantodomingo.com | €–€€*

THE SOUTHEAST

FINCA SALAMANCA
South of the village, this historic manor house lies in the middle of the grounds of a 5-hectare avocado *finca*, which serves excellent food. The dining room is in the old grain store and everything from duck to tuna carpaccio tastes excellent. *Daily 1.30–4pm, 7–10pm | Ctra Güímar–El Puertito, Km1.5 | tel. 922 51 45 30 | hotelfincasalamanca.com | €€*

INSIDER TIP
Granary dining

AROUND GÜÍMAR

1 ARAFO
4km/5 mins north of Güímar on the TF-523
This untouristy village (pop. 5,000) 4km north of Güímar is a gem, with a laurel-shaded plaza and a small bar *(daily | €)*. 🞀 H4

2 EL PUERTITO DE GÜÍMAR
5km/10 mins east of Güímar on the TF-612
There may not be a beach but you can still swim! In the harbour of El Puertito, ladders allow you access to the water. There is also a small promenade with al fresco bars and restaurants where you can pick up a cool drink or some basic food. 🞀 H5

3 PORÍS DE ABONA
18km/20 mins south of Güímar on the TF-61/TF-1
Just 2,000 people live in this fishing village with its winding harbour promenade and small but good swimming beach. The view of the bay and delicious tapas at *Café al Mar (daily | C/ Martín Rodríguez 14 | €)* make the detour to Porís worthwhile. 🞀 H6

4 ARICO
35km/1 hr south of Güímar on the TF-28
This village (pop. 7,000) is made up of several sections which stretch along the main road. At *Arico Nuevo*, a Site of Special Historical Architectural Interest, beautifully preserved village houses line both sides of a sloping side road and there's a quiet plaza with chapel. It's all neatly whitewashed and the doors and window frames are painted in classic Canarian green – something of a rarity for Tenerife. 🞀 G6

EL MÉDANO

(🞀 G8) ★ **El Médano ("The Dune") is located 7km east of Reina Sofía airport and is home to Tenerife's longest natural beaches. The bright sand stretches for miles along the coast and is popular with bathers and surfers alike. The latter love the frequent strong winds here, which can put off more sedate holidaymakers …**

The village itself has a population of 3,000 and is extremely laid back – this

EL MÉDANO

Montaña Roja, "Red Mountain", rises above Playa de la Tejita

is still a place where the locals rule the roost over tourists. The broad Plaza Príncipe de Asturias is a place where people like to meet for a chat over a beer. There is good fish to be had too – fresh off the boats.

EATING & DRINKING

FLASHPOINT
A surfers' hangout on the seafront with a view of the water and the waves. Here you can relax with your wetsuit on. The sea breeze makes Flashpoint's burgers and fish curries all the more appetising. *Daily 9.30am–11pm | Paseo Marítimo 52 | tel. 922 17 61 11 | €€*

SPORT & ACTIVITIES

Quite a few surf schools have taken up residence in El Médano. The *Sunset Kite Center (Paseo Nuestra Señora de las Mercedes de Roja 24 | tel. 922 92 51 51 | sunsetkitecenter.com)* offers kitesurfing, surfing and wingfoil lessons for everyone for beginners to the more experienced.

BEACHES

Playa El Médano begins in the middle of the resort and is just over 2km long. Swimmers splash about near the shore – but be careful because the wind occasionally brings

THE SOUTHEAST

AROUND EL MÉDANO

5 LOS ABRIGOS
6km/6 mins west of El Médano on the TF-643

Sadly, this village (pop. 2,000) is scarred by ugly tower blocks. However, if you get down to the harbour, you will understand why tourists from all over the south flock here every day. Lining the promenade are several restaurants with beautiful sea views. Small and fairly basic, they serve excellent, simply prepared seafood literally fresh off the boats! The best sea view is from the narrow terrace of the *Perlas del Mar (Wed-Sun noon-11pm | tel. 922 17 00 14 | €€)*, at the tip of the small cape. Watch the boats sailing in and out while enjoying a plate of fresh fish, potatoes and *mojo* sauce. A small market is held every Tuesday from 6pm to 9pm. *G12*

kitesurfers uncomfortably close to the beach. Behind the beach is a volcano, the Montaña Roja, and beyond it the sandy *Playa de la Tejita* – a popular nudist spot – stretches towards Los Abrigos. To the north of El Médano there are rocky beaches at *Playa del Cabezo* and *Playa de la Jaquita*, which are popular with surfers (international surfing competitions are held here).

NIGHTLIFE

For sundowners, surfers head to the bars (such as *Flashpoint*) on the Plaza and on the promenade.

6 GRANADILLA
11.5km/10 mins north of El Médano on the TF-64

The centre of this little town set back from the coast has retained its old-school charm. The erstwhile *Convento de San Francisco* is today a cultural centre *(Mon-Fri | Centro de Cultura, Plaza González Mena)*. The old post office, next to the Baroque church of San Antonio de Padua, is now a smart hotel.

Casa Tagoro (Wed-Sun 6-11pm | C/ Tagoro 28 | tel. 922 77 22 40 | casa tagoro.com | €€-€€€) is the best place

AROUND EL MÉDANO

Paisaje Lunar: Canarian lunar landscape

for miles around for that special meal. A manor house with antique fixtures and fittings is the setting for the culinary creations conjured up by Karin and Gerhard Brodtrager. The menu takes its inspiration from both the Atlantic and the Alps; it features a varied tapas selection, plus some fantastic tasting menus. Even vegans are well catered for. *F7*

> **INSIDER TIP**
> The Atlantic meets the Alps

7 ITER
7km/5 mins east of El Médano on the TF-1

The *Instituto Tecnológico de Energías Renovables* (Institute for Renweable Energy) has an outdoor exhibition that explains photovoltaics and wind and geothermal energy. There are also 24 futuristic bioclimatic houses designed by architects from all over the world, who have managed to blend beautiful design with environmental innovation. Electricity comes from the wind and the sun, and water is produced in the centre's own desalination plant. The design of the houses varies enormously: light sun-catching cubes are next to bunkers dug into the earth, and playful curves contrast with hard angles. You can stay in the houses but you will need a car (and earplugs!)

> **INSIDER TIP**
> Construction with a clear conscience

THE SOUTHEAST

Polígono Industrial de Granadilla | tel. 922 74 77 58 | casas.iter.es | €€ | G7

VILAFLOR

(E-F6) **If you drive into the national park from the south, you'll pass through this somewhat sleepy village (pop. 3,000).**

Vilaflor, among the highest municipalities in Spain, stands at 1,400m above sea level, and is surrounded by terraced fields, where local farmers cultivate vines and vegetables. One small business bottles spring water under the brand names of *Pinalito* and *Fuente Alta*, which is drunk everywhere on Tenerife. Some women here still top up their income by making traditional *rosetas*, delicate lace rosettes, which are sewn on to blankets and shawls. You can find the lace on sale in the souvenir shops on the church square, where the women will happily demonstrate their extremely time-consuming art.

The area just above the town is known for its Canary pine forests. One famous example of the species is the 60m Pino Gordo; it is said that you will be lucky in love if you hug its trunk. It's by the TF-21 road that winds its way up to Mount Teide, passing some stunning viewpoints on the way. Another local curiosity is the ★ *Paisaje Lunar* (G8), 20km northeast of Vilaflor. This "lunar landscape" is a bizarre volcanic formation unique to the Canaries. You can only get there on foot (the PR-TF 72 trail) either from Vilaflor's church square *(13km/5 hrs there and back)* or on a slightly longer route departing from Km66 of the TF-21.

INSIDER TIP: Tree-mendous height

EATING & DRINKING

CASA PANA
Canarian home-style cooking in a rustic setting is on offer in this traditional house on the church square. You can also dine in the garden under the pomegranate tree. *Tue–Sun noon–5pm | C/ C Castaños 7 | tel. 922 70 90 70 | €€*

SLEEP WELL IN THE SOUTHEAST

AS NATURE INTENDED
Hotel Playa Sur (75 rooms | C/ La Gaviota s/n | tel. 922 17 61 20 | hotelplayasur.es | €€) in El Médano is located on Tenerife's longest-standing naturist beach, with a surf school right next door. The atmosphere is friendly, and the prices remain very reasonable. There are Balinese-style sunbeds by the pool.

MOUNTAIN HIGH
If you prefer fresh mountain air and easy access to the national park, then *Hotel Spa Villalba (27 rooms | Ctra San Roque s/n | tel. 922 70 99 30 | hotelvillalba.com | €€)* in Vilaflor may be just the place.

THE SOUTHWEST

TOTAL TOURISM

Most tourists think of the southwest when they think of Tenerife. This is where you'll find the finest beaches and where sunshine is practically guaranteed. Infrastructure here has developed to meet the needs of package tourism: hotels range from affordable to super-luxury, and there are shopping centres, restaurants from around the world, and more water sports and golf courses than anyone could possibly want.

The resort of Los Gigantes is named after the gigantic cliffs

You can walk through dramatic ravines or take a boat trip to look for whales or to head over to La Gomera – Tenerife's "little sister".

The change here has been so rapid that it has effectively wiped out traditional life. Farms have been sold and their fields lie fallow. The south has got rich off tourism and many locals live from it – indeed in this dry region there is almost no alternative.

THE SOUTHWEST

Los Gigantes ★ p.116

TF-38 (the approach to Teide)

Playa de la Arena ★

The huge cliffs of Los Gigantes soar to 600m above sea level ensuring that the stretch of coast all the way from the harbour to Punta de Teno remains undeveloped. It's best explored by boat!

10 Guía de Isora

8 Playa de Alcalá

9 San Juan

The Teide massif shields the south of the island from the cloud brought in on the trade winds, so it's nearly always sunny.

OCÉANO ATLÁNTICO

MARCO POLO HIGHLIGHTS

★ **BARRANCO DEL INFIERNO**
A gorge that leads to a waterfall and keeps getting greener the further you go ▶ p.114

★ **LOS GIGANTES**
Truly gigantic cliffs tower above the village ▶ p.116

★ **PLAYA DE LA ARENA**
This beach with jet-black sand is an extraordinary sight ▶ p.117

7 Playa Paraíso

La Caleta 3

Playa del Duque

Costa Adeje p.107

Playa de las Américas p.107

Playa del Camisón

Rows of hotels, popular beaches, calm seas, wellness resorts and lots of activities – holiday central!

2 La Gomera

40km, 40 mins

The neighbouring island of La Gomera is within touching distance. Ferries shuttle between Los Cristianos and San Sebastián de la Gomera several times a day.

LOS CRISTIANOS

(*E8*) **At first sight Los Cristianos, the oldest resort in the south, is pretty depressing: ugly hotels, terrible traffic and hardly any trees. However, the local council has pulled the emergency brakes and started to give the place a facelift. Traffic-calming schemes have been implemented, roads have been lined with palms and promenades smartened up, much to the delight of the many holidaymakers who enjoy coming to Los Cristianos because it still has local life.**

It has also become popular for people with disabilities because the beaches, restaurants and infrastructure have been adapted for a wide range of needs. The *Spa & Sport Mar y Sol* (see p. 119) is the only completely wheelchair-accessible resort on the Canaries.

The beach promenade links the new and old parts of the town. The beach teems with swimmers, further out in the bay fishing boats and ferries come in and out of their docks. Walkers almost unwittingly end up in the part of the town above the harbour, which, with its narrow alleys and tiny courtyards, serves as a reminder that the now-bustling seaside resort was once a quiet village.

EATING & DRINKING

EL CINE
One of the town's oldest restaurants tucked away in a small alley close to the promenade. It serves simple, authentic food, as it always has. Choice is limited, which means everything is fresh. That said, the traditional wrinkly potatoes *(papas arrugadas)* with *mojo* sauce are always on the menu. *Wed–Sun noon–11pm | C/ Juan Bariajo 8 | tel. 609 10 77 58 | €–€€*

LA FORTUNA NOVA
The sumptuous three-course set menus in *La Fortuna Nova* cost just 14 euros for lunch (a little more in the evening) and can be enjoyed on the shady terrace or in the quaint dining room. A sample menu may include warm Camembert with blueberries, hearty goulash, and panna cotta for dessert. Unbeatable value for money. *Closed Sun | C/ del Valle Menéndez 16 | tel. 922 79 51 92 | €*

MESÓN CASTELLANO
More Castilian than Canarian: you sit, surrounded by hunting trophies, lots of wood and wrought-iron chandeliers, while Señor Manuel José serves excellent meat dishes, often barbecued, plus wine from the mainland. *Mon–Sat 1–11pm | Av. Antonio Domínguez 40, El Camisón | tel. 922 79 21 36 | IG: restaurantemesoncastellano | €€*

PICCOLO
As the name suggests, it's all about antipasti, Roman-style pasta and daily Italian specials – on a terrace

THE SOUTHWEST

Palm trees, old boats and apartment blocks at Los Cristianos

overlooking the sea above Playa de las Vistas. *Daily 1pm–midnight | Av. Habana 11 | tel. 922 79 67 88 | FB | €€*

SHOPPING

ARTENERIFE 🌿
Island crafts are sold from a kiosk on the seafront. The artisans also exhibit and sell their work at open-air fairs. *Paseo Las Vistas | artenerife.com/kiosko-los-cristianos*

LIBRERÍA BÁRBARA
Bookshop with new and second-hand titles in lots of languages, plus maps and guidebooks. Run by a mother and daughter team. *Mon–Fri 10am–1.30pm and 4.30–8pm, Sat 10am–1.30pm | C/ Juan Pablo Abril 6 | libreriabarbara.com*

MERCADILLO
At the popular Sunday flea market *(rastro)* between Arona Gran Hotel and the beach, you'll find a lot of kitsch counterfeit objects, but also, occasionally, beautiful craftwork. *Sun 9am–2pm*

SPORT & ACTIVITIES

Here in the south virtually every sport imaginable is on offer: squash, golf, trampolining, hang-gliding, hiking, cycling, climbing, sailing, windsurfing, jet skiing, scuba diving, deep-sea fishing and much more.

To find out what exactly is on offer, take a walk along the beach, around the harbours and in the shopping malls and talk to the various agencies or pick their leaflets up in the tourist information office at Playa de las Vistas.

LOS CRISTIANOS

BOAT TRIPS
A gently rocking boat, the sea breeze and the possibility of spotting dolphins? Tourist boats offering a variety of entertainment set sail from the harbour every day when the sea is calm.

There are more than 25 species of whale and dolphin off Tenerife's coast and the chances of spotting them on a whale-watching tour are good; pilot whales and bottlenose dolphins are the most common. Information and tickets are available at the end of the promenade just by the harbour. *Mar de Ons | tel. 922 75 15 76 | mardeonstenerife.com*

CAMEL PARK
Camel rides are available from *La Camella*, an inland village. *Daily 10am–3.30pm | rides (20 mins) cost 22 euros per person, children 11 euros, animal finca 3 euros | getting there: TF-51 Km3.5 (free buses available from the south) | tel. 922 72 11 21 | camelpark.es*

GOLF
Take your pick from five courses. The green fee for 18 holes is approx. 60 euros in the summer and about double that in the winter. The *Amarilla Golf & Country Club (getting there: Autopista del Sur, Los Abrigos exit, Km3 | tel. 922 73 03 19 | amarillagolf.es)* has 18 holes, a nine-hole course and a putting course, plus riding stables, tennis courts and swimming pools.

Golf del Sur (getting there: Autopista del Sur, Los Abrigos exit, Km4 | tel. 922 73 81 70 | golfdelsur.es) has 27 holes, plus a golf academy.

Golf Center Los Palos (getting there: Autopista del Sur, Guaza exit, Km1.5 | tel. 922 16 90 80 | golflospalos.com) is an attractive nine-hole course offering golf classes for players at all levels.

THE SOUTHWEST

BEACHES

All the beaches have showers, toilets and first-aid stations.

PLAYA DE LOS CRISTIANOS
Great for volleyball, pedalos and sunbathing. This broad 1km-long beach starts right next to the harbour, meaning the water might not necessarily be clean. The area to the south of Los Cristianos is popular with nudists.

PLAYA DE LAS VISTAS
This bright and broad beach is protected by breakwaters meaning you can almost always swim here. There is an eye-catching fountain set against the green backdrop of the promenade. Wooden planks take you down to the water and there are lots of lifeguards around (who also help disabled people into the water).

NIGHTLIFE

What nightlife there is is concentrated around the promenade. Just off the *Playa de las Vistas* (enter from Av. de Habana), there are a number of cocktail bars. Music concerts are performed at the *Auditorio Infanta Leonor* (Av. Juan Carlos I 20 | arona.org/auditorio).

FESTIVALS & EVENTS

There is hardly a month without a festival in Los Cristianos and the Arona area. It starts with *Carnaval* in February/March, followed by *Arona Fashion Week* in May, the modern *ARN Culture Pride* in June and the more traditional boat processions to honour Carmen, the patron saint, at the start of September.

There are small folk festivals in the winter at the weekend, when

Dolphins almost always greet boat tours with an acrobatic display

AROUND LOS CRISTIANOS

Bahía del Duque, a posh resort on the Costa Adeje

musicians and dancers parade along the promenade.

AROUND LOS CRISTIANOS

1 COSTA DEL SILENCIO

12km/10 mins from Los Cristianos on the TF-655/TF-66

"Coast of Silence" – this is not the most fitting name for the southernmost point of Tenerife. Planes land at the nearby airport almost every minute during the high season. And the landscape beyond the town isn't particularly attractive: banana plantations behind high walls and expanses of plastic sheeting protecting the fields of vegetables don't exactly scream beauty.

The former fishing port of Las Galletas still has a small promenade with fish restaurants, such as the basic *La Marina (Fri-Wed noon-10pm | €-€€)* and the slightly smarter French-inspired *Le Grand Bleu (daily | €-€€)* 📖 *E-F8*

2 LA GOMERA

40km/50 mins west of Los Cristianos (by ferry)

Several times a day the *Fred Olsen Express* hydrofoil *(return from 90 euros/pers. | tel. 902 10 01 07 | fredolsen.es)* whisks passengers from Los

THE SOUTHWEST

Cristianos harbour across to the neighbouring island of La Gomera (journey time approx. 50 mins) – a great spot for a day trip. A similar ferry service is offered by the *Naviera Armas* shipping company *(tel. 902 45 65 00 | naviera armas.es).* 🕮 0

PLAYA DE LAS AMÉRICAS/ COSTA ADEJE

(🕮 D-E 7–8) **The northern edge of Los Cristianos seamlessly merges into the tourist citadel of** *Playa de las Américas***, which in turn becomes the smarter** *Costa Adeje* **and** *Bahía del Duque* **resorts further north. A set of great beaches, protected by breakwaters come "with all the trimmings", making this a great place for a holiday.**

Beyond the promenade are the hotels, apartment complexes, shopping malls (with travel agencies) and restaurants whose northern European cuisine will have you feeling right at home … But don't worry, there are a couple of Spanish restaurants too. While Playa de las Américas has seen better days, Costa Adeje, and even more so Bahía del Duque, is calmer and prettier. The five-star hotels there court a wealthy clientele, but their beaches are open to the public. You can take whale-watching trips (among others) from the yacht harbour at Puerto Colón.

SIGHTSEEING

PASEO MARÍTIMO ✪
There are virtually no traditional tourist sights here but a walk along the pleasantly shady promenade is a decent substitute. It runs for 12km along the coast. You can even walk all the way to La Caleta. And if you get tired along the way, stop off at a beach bar. In the shade of palm trees or canvas sails, you can gaze out to sea and enjoy cool drinks. Great options include the *OA Beach Club (see p. 112)* in front of the Hotel Villa Cortés, the *Papagayo Beach Club (see p. 108)*, and the *Monkey Beach Club* in Costa Adeje.

TOURIST TRAIN 👫
Had enough of walking? The tourist train will take you on a leisurely tour through the streets of Los Cristianos and Playa de las Américas. *Daily 10am–10pm | 9 euros, children 5 euros | departure: corner of Av. R Puig Lluvina/Av. Santiago Puig | touristic traintenerife. com*

EATING & DRINKING

BIANCO
Bianco, with its elegant, all-white aesthetic, is located close to the Safari shopping centre on Américas' Milla de Oro ("Golden Mile"), where a water show takes place every evening. The restaurant serves fine Italian cuisine, and there are heaters on the terrace in winter. *Daily 1.30–midnight | C.C. Safari, Av. de las Américas 5 | tel. 822 62 11 35 | biancorestaurant tenerifecom | €€*

PLAYA DE LAS AMÉRICAS/COSTA ADEJE

Mon–Fri 8am–11.30pm | Av. V Centenario 1 | tel. 922 75 07 13 | €–€€

LA CASITA DE TABY
This little tapas bar is hidden away in a shopping mall. The passionate owners, Taby and Manuel, serve up a wide selection of Spanish home cooking – from potato salad to cheese and *jamón* platters and squid. Atmospheric in the evening with the artfully lit promenade. The rooftop terrace is nice and airy. *Wed–Sun 6–11.45pm | Av. V Centenario 2 (1st floor Centro Comercial Paraíso, near Magma Center) | tel. 651 98 87 57 | €–€€*

PAPAGAYO BEACH CLUB
Excellent location on the promenade under palm trees with the sound of waves crashing in the background. Glistening white interior design with a wide choice of cocktails and snacks served all day long. DJ sessions and live flamenco organised in the evenings several times a week. *Daily 11am–3am, weekends until 6am | Paseo Marítimo/Av. Rafael Puig Lluvina | on the border with Costa Adeje | tel. 922 78 89 16 | papagayo beachclub.com | €*

EL GOMERO
A simple, rustic restaurant serving a wide range of good Canarian dishes, including squid and paella, with gofio mousse for pudding – all at very affordable prices. Also does good-value lunch menus.

INSIDER TIP: Canarian fast food

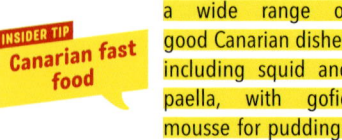

RADIO SABICH
Street food at its best: the menu may be small but all the food is freshly prepared on site, including the eponymous sabich, a flatbread filled with roasted aubergine, tomatoes, eggs, tahini and spicy sauce. And why "Radio"? Because the customers can choose the music! *Mon–Sat 12.30–3.30pm, 6.30–9.45pm | Av. Rafael Puig*

THE SOUTHWEST

Lluvina 6 (close to the seafront) | tel. 662 42 46 51 | radiosabich.com | €–€€

SHOPPING

There are plenty of malls *(centros comerciales* or *C.C.)* with outlets selling everything from kitschy keepsakes to tasty edible souvenirs.

ARTENERIFE

The state-run handicrafts chain has a stall at Playa de Troya that looks like the sawn-off hull of a ship. You're guaranteed to find Canarian products here and each item is unique. *Mon–Fri 10am–8.30pm, Sat 10am–1pm | Av. del Litoral; there is another Artenerife shop at the western end of Playa de las Vistas*

SIAM MALL

A free bus will take you to the beautiful and exotically stylish shopping mall next to Siam Park. You'll find more here than just the normal brand names (Mango, Zara etc.); there are also fine local retailers. Park your kids in the playground and your car in the free car park. *Daily 9.30am–6.30pm | Av. Siam 3 | free shuttle from several hotels every 30 mins | ccsiammall.com*

Playa de las Américas' promenade

PLAYA DE LAS AMÉRICAS/COSTA ADEJE

SPORT & ACTIVITIES

There's a wide range of outdoor activities here, as in the neighbouring town of Los Cristianos.

AQUALAND

A saltwater theme park with pools, water slides and flumes, waterfalls and a lazy river, so you can drift gently through the whole complex. There is also a dolphinarium with daily shows. *Daily 10am–5pm | admission 32 euros, children (3–4 years) 13 euros, (5–10 years) 24 euros | San Eugenio Alto | Autopista del Sur, exit 29 | aqualand.es/tenerife*

BOAT TRIPS & DIVING EXCURSIONS

Puerto Colón's harbour is the centre of the local diving and pleasure boat scene. Two-hour whale-watching trips can be booked, for example on the ❂ *Bonadea (tel. 618 13 27 29 | bonadea2catamaran.com)* from 50 euros. The "ecological tours" head to the Teno-Rasca Marine Strip, three nautical miles off the coast, where the Atlantic is 1,000m deep and the probability of seeing marine mammals is high. It's 39 euros for an excursion on the double-masted *Shogun (tel. 922 79 80 44 | atlanticoexcursiones.com)*. *Royal Delfín (from 58 euros | tel. 922 75 00 85 | tenerifedolphin.com | tenerifedolphin.com)* organises daily boat tours to Los Gigantes and Masca.

GOLF

The 18-hole *Golf Las Américas* course *(getting there: TF-1, exit 28 | tel. 922 75 20 05 | golflasamericas.com)* is located on 90 hectares of land near the resort. Green fee: 70–118 euros depending on the season, online booking possible.

The 27-hole *Costa Adeje Golf (Finca de los Olivos | getting there: TF-1 to Guía de Isora, exit to La Caleta | tel. 922 71 00 00 | golfcostaadeje.com)* is a verdant oupost in its desert environs. Green fee: from 68 euros for an 18-hole game. The course has a golf school and a driving range.

SIAM PARK ❂

Inspired by the architecture of Thailand, Siam Park sees itself as a "Kingdom of Water". Extending over an area of 14 hectares, there are temples, dragons and a market on stilts, as well as eight waterslides – one of which whooshes you through a shark tank. At a sandy artificial beach a wave machine churns out breakers up to 3m high. *Daily 10am–5pm (allow for long queues) | admission 42 euros, children 30 euros, combined ticket with Loro Parque 58/39.50 euros | Autopista del Sur, exit 28 | free buses from many of the hotels, daily 9.30am–6.30pm, every 30 mins | siampark.net.*

WELLNESS

THALASSO & SPA

What makes the *Mare Nostrum Spa (daily 10am–7pm | tel. 922 75 75 40 | marenostrumresort.com, Rubrik Wellness & Spa)* in the Mare Nostrum Resort so special is its charming setting and many different physiotherapy,

THE SOUTHWEST

A taste of Thailand at the Siam Water Park

beauty and spa treatments across a huge site.

The *Aqua Club Termal (daily 9am–10pm | C/ Calicia | tel. 922 97 92 87 | aquaclubtermal.com)* in Torviscas Alto has a spa with hydro massage, Roman spa, seawater pool, sauna and much more. It costs 33 euros for 2 hours (cheaper rates from 8–10pm). Massage, lymph drainage and other special treatments are extra.

Spa Sensations (daily 9am–9pm | inerostar.com) in the Hotel El Mirador has the most beautiful ambience. Bathe in a minimalist-styled thalasso pool with massaging water jets or in an enormous jacuzzi. Other features include treatment showers, hot-and-cold contrast pools and a hammam. As the name suggests there is a Southeast Asian theme to many of the treatments. Physiotherapists give Ayurvedic, Thai and yoga massages using natural oils and essences. The buffet breakfast and spa bundle is a bargain at 40 euros!

INSIDER TIP
Ancient treatments

BEACHES

Beneath the promenade at Playa de las Américas and Costa Adeje, many small beaches have been created, all with fine, golden sand, and

PLAYA DE LAS AMÉRICAS/COSTA ADEJE

protected from the surf by breakwaters, meaning they are safe for children. From *Playa de Troya* in the south to *Playa La Pinta* beyond Puerto Colón, one beach follows another. The beaches further north are quieter and have more space.

PLAYA DEL CAMISÓN
At the very southern tip of Tenerife, this golden gem of a beach lies at the foot of a palm-lined slope and has a view over Los Cristianos. Near the promenade, there is no traffic but plenty of cool beach bars to cater to the sun worshippers. Walk a bit further along the coastal promenade and you will come to a very popular spot. At sunset, people flock from miles around to enjoy a cocktail at *OA Beach Club (daily | €-€€)* by the Villa Cortés hotel. From here you can look out to the island of La Gomera while you relax with a drink at the end of a long day. The peace will only be broken by surfers trying to catch one final wave.

INSIDER TIP Sunset with style

PLAYA DEL DUQUE
The finest beach is also the furthest north. "Duke's Beach", 600m of pale sand with blue and white changing cabins, is overlooked by some rather grand hotels.

PLAYA DE FAÑABÉ
In a quiet resort of the same name, this 800m beach is ideal for relaxed swimming and sunbathing. The *Seasoul Lounge (daily from 1pm | Iberostar Hotel Anthelia)* means you don't need to miss out on the high life. Atop a slight slope at the north end of the beach, they offer cocktails and fresh fish to enjoy with their unbeatable sea view.

NIGHTLIFE

When the neon lights start to flicker on, treat yourself to an aperitif, take a stroll along the promenade or go for a bite to eat. Young people congregate in the *Verónica shopping centre (ccveronicas.com)*, the entertainment quarter, or along the main street near *Playa de Troya* – for example at the *Jumping Jacks (jumpingjackstenerife.com)*. The next generation up (i.e. over 20s), on the other hand, gather in the cool music pub, *Magic (live music daily from 10pm | Av. de las Américas | magicbartenerife.com)*.

The Pirámide de Arona, home to the *Hard Rock Café (hardrock.com/cafes/tenerife)*, has more live events. For information about the latest gay hangouts, consult *gaytenerife.net*.

CASINO PLAYA DE LAS AMÉRICAS
Games of chance – from blackjack to roulette – are on offer in the basement of the Hotel Gran Tinerfe. *Mon–Thu 8pm–3am, Fri–Sun 8pm–4am | admission free (bring ID) | Paseo Cándido García Sanjuan 2 | tel. 922 79 37 58 | casinostenerife.com)*.

MAGMA
Pop, classical and folk concerts are occasionally held in this avant-garde

THE SOUTHWEST

building near the motorway. *Av. de los Pueblos | TF-1, exit 28*

PIRÁMIDE DE ARONA
Before the Covid-19 pandemic, events staged in the auditorium of this imposing Las Vegas-style pyramid included ballet and flamenco evenings with the famous choreographer Carmen Mota. The plan is for these events to be revived, but for the moment it functions as a conference centre. Visits by appointment only. *Information kiosk, Av. de las Américas | tel. 922 75 75 49 | marenostrumresort.com*

AROUND PLAYA DE LAS AMÉRICAS/ COSTA ADEJE

3 LA CALETA
4 km/50 mins north of Las Américas (walking along the promenade)
Once a quiet fishing village with a view over the developing coast, La Caleta itself has long since been swallowed up by tourism. Its posh

Shimmering blue sea, fine sand, pine trees and parasols: Playa del Duque

AROUND PLAYA DE LAS AMÉRICAS/COSTA ADEJE

hotels and golf course provide plenty of evidence, as does the car-free promenade which you can use to walk to Los Cristianos.

La Caleta's fish restaurants have largely survived, even if rustic dives have been transformed into large, comfortable restaurants. Many people come to La Caleta solely for the good food – the former fishing village has developed into the gastronomic gem of the south coast. You can enjoy fine seafood – ceviche with citrus cocktail, squid carpaccio, tempura shrimp with vegetables – and a sea view from the terrace at *Mirlo (daily noon–midnight | C/el Muelle 7 | tel. 822 90 43 67 | €€€)*. Next door, the equally scenic terrace restaurant *La Masía del Mar* and *Piscis (daily noon –11pm | C/ del Muelle 3 | tel. 922 71 08 95 | masiadelmar.com | €€)* has an equally good reputation: the delicious fish soup is served in small copper pots, and you can pick your fish from their tanks.

INSIDER TIP: The freshest fish around

Looking for a truly exceptional meal? Awarded a Michelin star, *El Rincón de Juan Carlos (Tue–Sat evenings only, reservations required | Av. Virgen de Guadalupe 21 | tel. 922 86 80 40 | web.elrincondejuancarlos.com | €€€)* is located on the "promenade deck" of the five-star Royal Hideaway Hotel. The Padrón family creates creative Canarian dishes that are both delicious and visually appealing. Instead of an à la carte menu, it offers a three-hour tasting menu – 12 courses for €170, plus six glasses of matching wine for €90. *D7*

4 ADEJE
7km/10 mins north of Las Américas on the TF-1

Most visitors just pass through this sleepy place on their way to "Hell's Gorge" *(Barranco del Infierno)*. However, it is a very interesting place in itself. At the beginning of the 16th century, Spanish conquerors built the church of *Santa Úrsula (C/ Grande)*, with its beautifully carved wooden ceiling. The stunning Baroque altar came later. The square outside is perhaps even more beautiful, serving as a kind of gateway to the gorge. It's a perfect spot to get a first glimpse of the huge Barranco del Infierno.

Local farmers come to sell their produce at the pleasant and relaxed *Agromercado (Wed 3–7pm, Sun 8am–2pm | C/ Archajara)*, where you can buy fruit, vegetables, goat's cheese, aniseed bread and much more. At the upper end of *Calle de los Molinos, Restaurante Otelo (Wed–Mon 11am–11pm | tel. 922 78 03 74 | otelorestaurante.com | €–€€)* boasts great views over Adeje. This is also the start of a beautiful walk into the ★ *Barranco del Infierno (daily 8.30am–4pm, until 5pm in winter, gorge open until 6pm, total hiking time approx. 3 hrs, 6.5km | admission 11 euros | access only with prior reservation online or at the information stand at the entrance to the gorge | barrancodelinfierno.es)*. Helmets are mandatory (can be hired) due to the danger of falling rocks. A former shepherd's path winds its way up into the exposed, barren mountains. Later as you approach the narrow, shaded "Hell's Gorge"

THE SOUTHWEST

Colourful woodcarving: altarpiece and ceiling in Adeja's Iglesia Santa Úrsula

with its meandering stream, the vegetation becomes less sparse. And when you reach the end of the gorge, you will find a waterfall that drops over 80m. *E7*

5 ARONA

8km/10 mins north of Las Américas on the TF-28/TF-51

Overshadowed by the huge Roque del Conde, it is hard to believe that this sleepy town is the administrative centre responsible for the two seemingly inexhaustible gold mines of Los Cristianos and Playa de las Américas. Very few of the many billions of euros spent in the Arona area ends up here, but it does boast an attractive town hall beside a square shaded by laurels and a church dating from 1627. *E7*

6 ÁGUILAS JUNGLE PARK

9km/10 mins northeast of Las Américas on the TF-1/TF-28

A jungle on Tenerife? Up above the resorts, 7 hectares of land have been turned into a patch of rainforest that includes lakes and waterfalls. You can watch eagles, vultures, falcons, owls and other raptors hunting (and being fed by their handler). There is also a cactus garden, climbing equipment, and pedal boats on a mini lake – enough to keep children entertained for a day. *Daily 10am–5.30pm | admission 32 euros, children (3–4 years) 13 euros, (5–10 years) 25 euros | getting there: Ctra Los Cristianos–Arona Km3 (TF-1, junction 27) | free buses from the resorts in the south | aguilasjunglepark.com | 3–4 hrs E7*

LOS GIGANTES

🞟 PLAYA PARAÍSO
11km/15 mins northwest of Las Américas (on the TF-1/TF-47)

The name "Paradise Beach" is a slight exaggeration. But there are two small sand bays which are great for swimming. The resort's eye-catcher is a twin tower: the *Hard Rock Hotel (624 rooms | Av. de Adeje | tel. 971 92 76 91 | hardrockhotels.com/tenerife | €€€)*. Its rooftop bar, *The 16th (daily from 6pm | Av. de Adeje | tel. 971 92 76 91 | hardrockhotels.com/tenerife)*, is chic and stylish. Up here on the large terrace you can enjoy the view along with live music (from blues to funk) most evenings. *▯ D7*

> **INSIDER TIP**
> **A cool place to cool down**

LOS GIGANTES

(▯ C5) This was once the small fishing village of Puerto de Santiago. But the tourism boom added two new developments to it: Playa de la Arena is named after its beach, and ★ Los Gigantes, to the north, after the "gigantic" cliffs that rise 450m from the waves. The marvellous landscape stands in contrast with row upon row of giant, identikit hotels.

The coastal road comes to an end at *Los Gigantes*. The resort shares its name with the cliffs, which is fitting as

Modern and historic boats anchor at Los Gigantes marina

THE SOUTHWEST

the steep streets cling on to them for dear life. The place to be here is *Poblado Marinero* marina, where yachts bob around in front of the dramatic backdrop.

EATING & DRINKING

RESTAURANTE PANCHO
This beach restaurant at Playa de la Arena offers fine cuisine and has won several awards. While there are good meat dishes (e.g. honey-cooked duck breast), the focus is on fish. Start with shrimp salad, tuna carpaccio, or smoked fish, followed by grouper casserole or grilled turbot. Hake *(merluza)* alone is served in four variations: grilled and steamed, in green sauce, and *à la romana* (i.e. in crispy breadcrumbs). The desserts are also impressive: how about fig ice cream topped with chocolate sauce? *Mon–Sat 1–4pm and 8–10pm, Sun 1–4pm | Av. Marítima 26 | tel. 922 86 13 23 | restaurantepancho.es | €€€*

SPORT & ACTIVITIES

BOAT TRIPS
The best way to see Los Gigantes is from the water. The yacht *Carolin Sophie*, which also offers dolphin-watching trips, is just one of a number of boats that bring sightseers close to the cliffs *(daily from 11.30am | 2-hr trip 30 euros | 100m from the harbour entrance on the right | tel. 922 86 03 32)*. The catamaran *Nashiro Uno* also organises one- to three-hour whale- and dolphin-watching tours from the *harbour (daily 11am, 1pm and 3pm | from 35 euros, depending on duration | tel. 922 86 19 18 | maritima acantilados.com).*

BEACHES

PLAYA DE LA ARENA ★
A truly beautiful place with 300m of jet-black volcanic sand contrasting with the bright green palm trees. The beach is the island's sunniest spot and has regularly been awarded the European Blue Flag for the cleanliness of its water and sand. It also has excellent facilities with sun loungers (to hire), toilets and lifeguards.

PLAYA DE LOS GUÍOS
The big beach at Playa de los Guíos starts at the Poblado Marinero marina. A great location under the cliffs is also a reason for caution due to falling rocks; make sure you pick a spot nearer the water!

AROUND LOS GIGANTES

8 PLAYA DE ALCALÁ
6km/10 mins south of Los Gigantes on theTF-47
The luxurious *Palacio de Isora* hotel in Alcalá is the sort of place that other hotels look up to. This large complex in southern Spanish style is situated by a rocky beach with distant views of La Gomera. The fishing village around it with its simple houses and pretty harbour seems to belong to a

AROUND LOS GIGANTES

The views are amazing along the TF 38 between Teide National Park and Chío

completely different (and bygone) world. 📖 *C6*

9 SAN JUAN

8.5km/12 mins south of Los Gigantes on the TF-47
The luxury *Ritz Carlton Abama* resort emerges from San Juan like a rusty mirage and looks like a Moroccan fort. It even has its own golf course. There are villa complexes on several levels running right down to the sea. With a park, seven pools, a spa and a funicular down to the bright beach below, it's simply the best.

From the road San Juan appears somewhat dull but if you head to the harbour, you'll see it has retained some of its former charm with an attractive artificial sandy beach, promenade and lots of restaurants. 📖 *C6*

10 GUÍA DE ISORA

16km/26 mins southeast of Los Gigantes on the TF-454 and TF-82
Many resort employees live in cheap, makeshift buildings in this village. If you want to see the more attractive side of Guía de Isora (pop. 5,200) head to the historical centre above the main road. The handsome *Iglesia Nuestra Señora de la Luz* on the church square is a reminder that much wealth was created here in the 16th century. 📖 *D6*

THE SOUTHWEST

🕚 TF-38 (THE APPROACH TO TEIDE)

Chío is a rather drab settlement but it's an unavoidable transit point for visitors to Teide National Park approaching from the west. The TF-38, one of three access roads to the national park, begins just north of town. It's a stunning drive that leads first through farmland and then into the volcanic region at 2,000m, which is almost devoid of vegetation. A good place to stop en route is the *Mirador de las Narices del Teide*. You could also make a short detour to the pottery museum at Arguayo (see p. 61) by turning off the TF-38 just ten minutes' drive north of Chío. *D5*

SLEEP WELL IN THE SOUTHWEST

ALL-INCLUSIVE, BUT A BIT DIFFERENT

Even Letizia, the Spanish Queen, has recognised the exemplary facilities at this hotel, which is arguably the best in Europe for people with disabilities. Every part of the 🍃 *Spa & Sport Mar y Sol (160 rooms | Av. Amsterdam 8 | tel. 922 75 05 40 | marysol.org | €€)* in Los Cristianos is accessible, from the thermal pool with its assisted entry to the sport's hall, diving school and golf course. An all-inclusive hotel in the best sense of the word: it's inclusive for everyone, whether they have a disability or not.

HELLO ALOE

The aloe plant, which thrives in the Canarian climate, is the inspiration for the design, the cuisine and the spa treatments at the adult-only, beachfront *Iberostar Selection Sábila (472 rooms | Av. Ernesto Sartí 5 | Costa Adeje | tel. 922 71 23 00 | iberostar.com | €€€)*. Everywhere is decorated in a soothing shade of green; aloe smoothies and detox teas are served, and there are pools where you can bathe in extracts from the "wonder plant".

DISCOVERY TOURS

Want to get under the skin of the island? Then our discovery tours are the ideal guide – they provide advice on which sights to visit, tips on where to stop for that perfect holiday snap, a choice of the best places to eat and drink, and suggestions for fun activities.

Mount Teide bugloss blooms despite the arid conditions

DISCOVERY TOURS: AN OVERVIEW

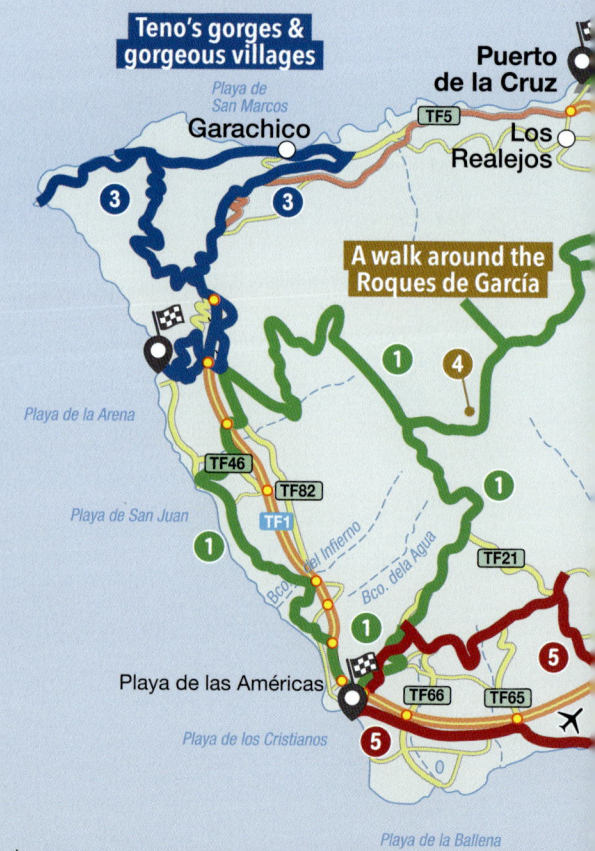

❶ TENERIFE IN TWO DAYS

- Admire the magnificent buildings in La Orotava and La Laguna
- Learn about volcanology in the El Portillo visitor centre
- Spain's highest mountain
- Stunning "lunar landscape" and crystal-clear air
- Strings of beaches in different shades
- Check out the view from the "Queen's Shoe"
- Discover science-fiction architecture in no-man's land
- Enjoy amazing views from the island's "spine"

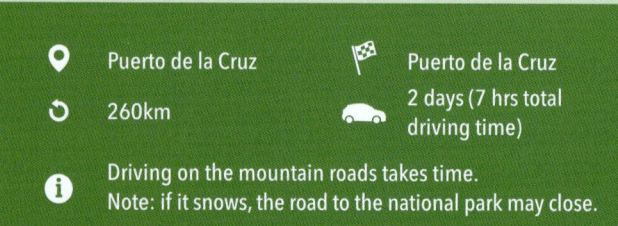

📍 Puerto de la Cruz	🏁 Puerto de la Cruz
⟳ 260km	🚗 2 days (7 hrs total driving time)

ℹ️ Driving on the mountain roads takes time.
Note: if it snows, the road to the national park may close.

DAY 1 — ATTRACTIVE AND ATMOSPHERIC

❶ **Puerto de la Cruz**
 7km 10 mins
❷ **La Orotava**

 26.5km 27 mins

It is worth setting off early because the busiest time in the national park and on the Teide cable car is around midday. Start in ❶ **Puerto de la Cruz ➤ p. 42** and *head south* through the densely populated **Valle de La Orotava ➤ p. 50**, first to the picturesque village of ❷ **La Orotava ➤ p. 50**, where romantic plazas, churches and monasteries serve as reminders of the island's colonial past. *Carry on along the TF-21. Above Aguamansa* is **La Caldera ➤ p. 54**, the green crater which is now a picnic area and starting point for hiking tours into the pine forest. Between Km22 and 23, stop to take a look at **La Margarita de Piedra**, a large naturally formed basalt rosette, remnant of the era when there was much volcanic activity here.

EL TEIDE PEAK IN THE NATIONAL PARK

At an altitude of 2,000m the forest thins and volcanic rock takes over. With an attractive visitor centre,

DISCOVERY TOURS

❸ **El Portillo ➤ p. 64** acts as the "gateway" to the Las Cañadas crater and the **Teide National Park ➤ p. 62**. A rock garden contains all the plants that have adapted to the extreme alpine climate; the finest is the Mount Teide bugloss, a sparking red perennial that grows to a height of about 2m. As you continue your journey, the road crosses lava and ash fields in white, green, red, grey and pitch black. They bear witness to the volcanic activity that formed the island millions of years ago. *At Km43, you'll reach the turn-off to the station for the cable car,* which, in just a few minutes, takes you from 2,300m to the ❹ **La Rambla summit station** at 3,555m, almost at the top of **Pico del Teide ➤ p. 64**. The view from the top is amazing.

❸ El Portillo
13km 15mins
❹ La Rambla summit station

FOLLOW THE CRATER

The next stop is at the **Roques de García ➤ p. 63**, giant, weathered rock formations that sit majestically above a plateau surrounded by jagged rocks. Take a break at the nearby ❺ **Parador Nacional ➤ p. 65**. Both its cafeteria and rustic yet elegant restaurant *(€–€€)* have impressive views of Mount Teide. There are also great views from the 5m-high Zapato de la Reina, or "Queen's Shoe", and the ❻ **Boca de Tauce**, a gap in the crater rim. *You now leave Las Cañadas crater and follow the TF-21 down through the sparse pine forest to* ❼ **Vilaflor ➤ p. 97**, a mountain village at an altitude of 1,400m. Enjoy a hearty meal at **Casa Pana ➤ p. 97** and maybe spend the night at the delightful **Hotel Spa Vilaflor ➤ p. 97**.

INSIDER TIP: Fit for a queen

8.5km 5 mins
❺ Parador Nacional
7km 7 mins
❻ Boca de Tauce
15.5km 15 mins
❼ Vilaflor

BUSY BEACHES, PEACEFUL FORESTS — DAY 2

While Vilaflor is often hidden in the clouds, the village of **Arona ➤ p. 115**, *just 12km away,* gets bathed in light from the south. You are now leaving the peace of the mountains and heading for the heart of Tenerife's tourism industry. *Drive down to the coast* where a 12km promenade links the resorts, from Los Cristianos to La Caleta, with beaches every few hundred metres. The best of them, ❽ **Bahía del Duque ➤ p. 107**, is

25km 25 mins
❽ Bahía del Duque

9 San Juan
23km   25 mins

10 Mirador de Chirche
16km   12 mins

surrounded by spectacular hotels. There are some excellent fish restaurants in La Caleta ➤ p. 114, but hold off until you reach **9** San Juan ➤ p. 118, a quiet fishing village with a row of harbour restaurants.

ROAD TRIP WITH A VIEW

After your meal, *take the TF-463* up to Chío, back to the island's magnificent natural surroundings. *On the TF-38*, you'll plunge into a beautiful volcanic landscape dotted with pine trees. From the **10** Mirador de Chirche (which has a restaurant), you can see the neighbouring western islands on clear days; while from the

DISCOVERY TOURS

⓫ **Mirador de Chío** you can look out across swathes of black volcanic debris to the **Pico Viejo** ➤ **p. 64**, Mount Teide's younger sister. At the **Boca de Tauce** you'll *rejoin the TF-21 mountain road*, which is so spectacular that you won't mind returning along it in the opposite direction. *On the way back turn onto the TF-24 – the "island's spine" – at El Portillo.* After a few kilometres, you'll pass the entrance to the futuristic **Observatorio del Teide** ➤ **p. 65**, and *at Km32* you will pass through the black, white and yellow rock formations known as **La Tarta** ("The Tart"). After that it's back into the pine forest. There are plenty of clearings with viewpoints offering vistas out to the east, northwest and occasionally over to the islands of La Palma and Gran Canaria.

⓫ Mirador de Chío

71.5km   1 hr 10 mins

SUNDOWNERS ON THE BEACH

After so much nature, it's now time for a spot of culture: ⓬ **La Laguna** ➤ **p. 77** is a picturesque town whose cobbled, pedestrianised streets are lined with churches, monasteries and palaces. A hearty meal can be enjoyed at **La Bourmet** ➤ **p. 79**. From La Laguna, *take the TF-5 motorway* back to ❶ **Puerto de la Cruz** ➤ **p. 42** for an early evening swim. The pitch-black **Playa Jardín** ➤ **p. 48** is the perfect place for a sunset dip. Then relax with a cocktail in one of the shady beach bars.

⓬ La Laguna

29.5km   22 mins

❶ Puerto de la Cruz

La Laguna is pristine and picturesque

❷ ANAGA'S LAUREL FORESTS & AN IDYLLIC BEACH

➤ Stop and stare from a series of ever-better viewpoints
➤ Learn about laurel
➤ Warm up with with a bowl of cress soup in the mountains …
➤ … or eat fresh fish on the coast
➤ Descend a series of switchbacks to the wild coast
➤ Round it off at the white Playa de las Teresitas
➤ Take in a sightseeing finale in the capital

📍 La Laguna
🏁 Santa Cruz de Tenerife
→ 86km
🚗 1 day (2 hrs total driving time)

ℹ️ From the north: From Puerto de la Cruz/La Orotava take the TF-5 (30 mins) to ❶ **La Laguna**.
From the south: take the TF-1 (1½ hrs) to ❶ **La Laguna**.

❶ La Laguna
8km 10 mins
❷ Mirador de Jardina
2.5km 2 mins
❸ Mirador Cruz del Carmen

ENJOY THE VIEWS
Start in ❶ **La Laguna** ➤ p. 77 and *take the beautiful TF-12 to Las Mercedes where the laurel forest begins. At Km25.1,* make a stop at the ❷ **Mirador de Jardina**, from where you can survey Mount Teide and over half the island. Soon after, *at Km22.7,* you will reach the ❸ **Mirador Cruz del Carmen** ➤ p. 85, where a well-camouflaged **visitor centre** will give you information about all the footpaths in the region. Even an hour's easy walking will give you a good sense of the laurel forest. Cruz del Carmen also has a tiny chapel and the rustic bistro **La Gangochera** ➤ p. 85, where almost everything is locally sourced. Try the cress soup.

INSIDER TIP Super soup

4km 4 mins
❹ Mirador Pico del Inglés

SWITCHBACKS
Continue along the road. The next viewpoint, at Km21.8, the ❹ **Mirador Pico del Inglés**, provides a different panorama over the northwest and northeast coasts. *If you turn off the TF-12 you can explore remote hamlets,*

DISCOVERY TOURS

such as Las Carboneras, Chinamada or Taborno. ❺ **Casas de Afur** is especially quaint *(fork left at Km18.4)*. *Back on the TF-12, continue along the high mountain road and at Km11.4 you'll reach a confusing junction.* A left turn would take you on the TF-123 to Bailadero, where sheep and goats were once herded. *However, you need to start your descent on the TF-12 (towards San Andrés). After 1km, take a left and go through a tunnel before joining the TF-134 towards Taganana/Benijo.* A series of switchbacks along sharply defined ridges provides magnificent views of the landscape and the cliffs below. There are not many places to stop and take photos until you reach ❻ **Taganana**.

BACK TO THE COAST

After this dizzying stretch, you've earned some seafood. On this rocky coastline restaurants offering great views of the wild sea can be found in Roque de las Bodegas – i.e. the authentic Canarian ❼ **Casa África** *(daily | Roque de las Bodegas 3 | tel. 922 59 01 00 | €-€€)*, where the friendly Señora África cooks up traditional specialities, and in ❽ **Benijo** with its pretty beach.

11km	11 mins
❺ Casas de Afur	
20km	19 mins
❻ Taganana	
9.5km	9 mins
❼ Casa África	
9.5km	9 mins
❽ Benijo	

LAST STOP: TOP BEACH

18km 18 mins
❾ San Andrés
12km 21 mins
❿ Santa Cruz de Tenerife

After visiting Benijo turn round and *head back uphill and, from the spine of the Anaga Mountains, follow the switchbacks down the TF-12 to the eastern side of island* and the fishing and seaside resort of ❾ San Andrés ➤ p. 76. If you're hungry, grab a bite to eat here and enjoy a swim at Tenerife's finest beach, the Playa de las Teresitas. *Now head along the coast to the capital* ❿ Santa Cruz de Tenerife ➤ p. 70. From there either head back to the north via La Laguna or take the TF-1 motorway back to your resort.

The original beach at Benijo in the northeast is only suitable for swimming at low tide

DISCOVERY TOURS

❸ TENO'S GORGES & GORGEOUS VILLAGES

- ➤ A detour for art fans to see a traditional pottery workshop
- ➤ Rugged mountains and a stunning village
- ➤ The lighthouse at the end of the island
- ➤ Buena Vista: a good view of steep cliffs
- ➤ Time travel and relaxation by the sea in Garachico
- ➤ The island's "thousand-year-old" resident

📍 Los Gigantes 🏁 Los Gigantes
🔄 110km 🚗 1 day (2 hrs total driving time)

ℹ Note: The TF-445 towards the Punta de Teno Nature Reserve is closed after it has rained and in high winds due to the risk of falling rocks; there is a shuttle *bus 369 (daily 10am–6pm | titsa.com)*.

WINDING MOUNTAIN ROADS

❶ **Los Gigantes** ➤ p. 116 are striking rocky cliffs which rise to 450m above the village of the same name, dwarfing its houses, boats and people. These "Giants", located at the southern end of the Teno Massif, give a foretaste of the inaccessible mountains where you will spend your day. *The TF-454 first climbs through hairpin bends on its way up to Santiago del Teide,* passing banana and tomato plantations. *At Km11, make a detour to* ❷ **Arguayo** ➤ p. 61, a traditional village known for its ceramics. Visitors are welcome to watch the skilled potters at work and purchase their products in an old, restored workshop.

WILD NATURE

After **Santiago del Teide** ➤ p. 61 the landscape becomes more dramatic: everywhere you look are steep cliffs, rugged rocks and hardy plants. Erosion has gnawed away at the volcanic rock of the **Teno Mountains** ➤ p.60, a very ancient geological

❶ Los Gigantes

14.5km 17 mins

❷ Arguayo

11km 10 mins

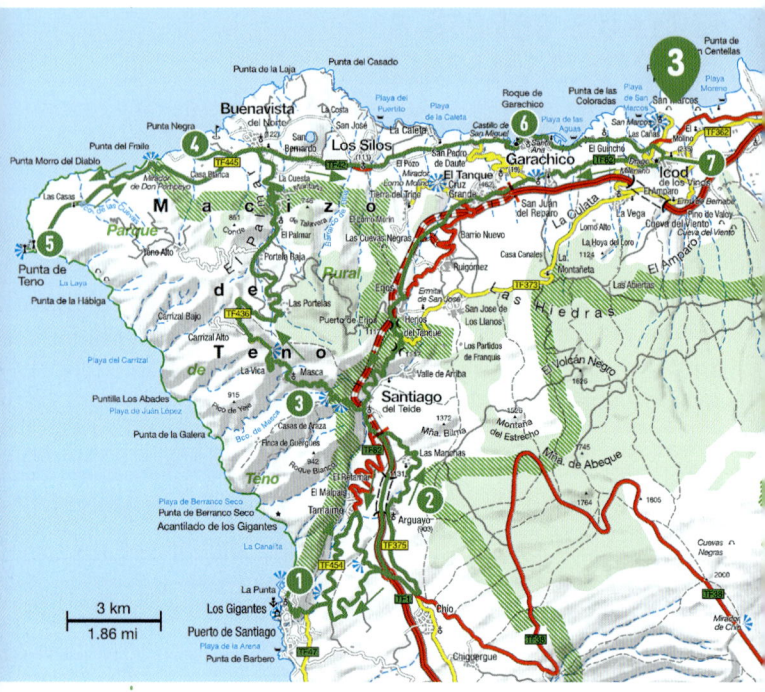

③ Masca

19km 21 mins

④ El Burgado

formation. From the **Mirador de Cherfe** you get your first glimpse of ③ **Masca** ➤ p. 61, a hamlet tucked between sheer rock walls, which was not joined up to the road network until the 1980s. It is divided between several rocky outcrops and a tour through this dispersed village will involve treading carefully on crooked cobblestones. It has several small restaurants. *For a few kilometres, the narrow road winds its way through the mountains.* The *Mirador de Hilda has a café and terrace and splendid views back up the Masca valley.* From the **Mirador de Baracán**, on the next pass, you'll have a view of the gentler hills in the north.

INSIDER TIP
Look behind you

ALONG THE STEEP CLIFFS
Drive through the village of Las Portelas and head down to **Buenavista del Norte** ➤ p. 59, where you can enjoy excellent seafood on the coast at ④ **El Burgado** *(daily |*

DISCOVERY TOURS

Playa de la Arena | tel. 922 12 78 31 | FB | €€). From Buenavista, you board the shuttle bus that takes you to the foot of the cliffs in Tenerife's far northwest (see information box). The journey comes to an end at ❺ **Punta de Teno ➤ p. 60**, where you can jump into the waves in a sheltered bay at the foot of the high cliffs. The lighthouse at the very tip of the island, built in 1897 and one of the Canary Islands' most beautiful, is also worth a look.

| 10km | 10 mins |
| ❺ Punta de Teno |
| 18.5km | 18 mins |

THOUSAND-YEAR-OLD TREE?

After so much wilderness, a bit of town-life might be in order. *Return to Buenavista and continue on the TF-42 for about 5 minutes until you reach* ❻ **Garachico ➤ p. 56**, where the old town – with fort, monastery and colonial houses – is a splendid example of Tenerife's traditional architecture. The volcanic coast is also worth a look – you can enjoy the view over a meal on the terrace of **El Caletón Chill Out** *(daily | Av. Tomé Cano | tel. 922 13 33 01 | €€)*. After your break, *continue on the TF-42 to* ❼ **Icod de los Vinos ➤ p. 54**, where you will

| ❻ Garachico |
| 5.5km | 5 mins |
| ❼ Icod de los Vinos |

Masca is a beautiful hamlet in a magnificent mountainous landscape

find the Drago Milenario, a dragon tree once believed to be 1,000 years old (but, in fact, "only" 500–600 years old) and one of Tenerife's most recognised landmarks. The streets here are pretty and lined with grand houses. Sample a glass of wine in one of the food shops. *Now head back in the direction of Puerto de Santiago along a less dramatic but equally beautiful mountain road through El Tanque, Erjos and Santiago del Teide to your starting point at* ❶ Los Gigantes ➤ p. 116.

50km 35 mins

❶ Los Gigantes

❹ A WALK AROUND THE ROQUES DE GARCÍA

- ➤ The top of the island
- ➤ Gigantic natural sculptures
- ➤ The site of the Battle of the Titans
- ➤ A white tower and a cathedral that's full of secrets
- ➤ What happened to the dinosaurs?
- ➤ The steep climb is worth the effort!

📍	Mirador de la Ruleta	🏁	Mirador de la Ruleta
⟳	4.5km	🚶	Total walking time 1¾ hrs
📶	Difficulty: medium	↗	Ascent: 110m

ℹ️ Bus: From Puerto de la Cruz take bus 348 at 9.30am to its final stop at the *Parador*; from Costa Adeje/Las Américas take bus 342. Return around 4pm.
Car: If you're driving, take the TF-21 to Km46.4. Park at the Mirador de la Ruleta. There's also a car park at the *Parador*. Don't leave anything in your car!

VIEW OVER THE PLATEAU

❶ Mirador de la Ruleta

From your starting point at the ❶ Mirador de la Ruleta, take a few steps in the *direction of the TF-21 and turn left immediately behind the group of rocks along a wide*

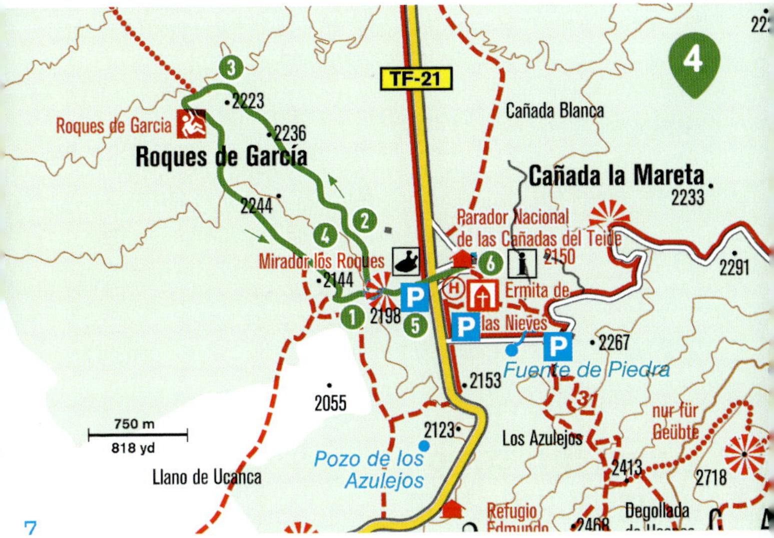

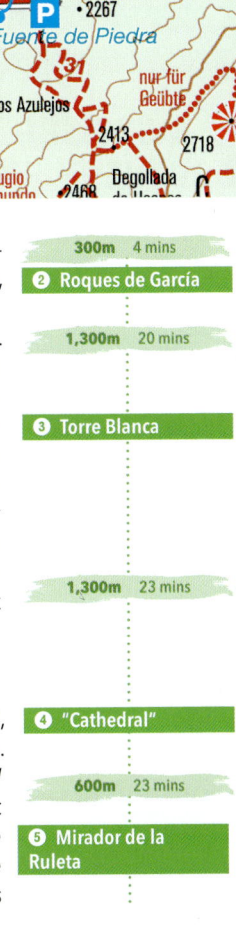

path signposted "Sendero 3". The path ascends gradually past the foot of the ❷ **Roques de García** ➤ p. 63, which have been sculpted into magnificent formations by wind and rain over the course of millions of years. The path soon narrows and follows the edge of an old lava field. *Thirty minutes after setting off, you'll pass the* ❸ **Torre Blanca** (White Tower), the last in the series of gigantic rock formations. A natural plateau has been carved out here offering a vast panoramic view over the Ucanca plain. *Shortly after the plateau, the path veers left down to the plain,* with the craggy foot of the Roques de García rising up in front of you. When the path becomes unclear, cairns have been used to mark the route.

NATURE'S ARCHITECTURE

You'll quickly spot your next destination, ❹ **"Cathedral"**, a 100m-high solitary rock rising up from the plateau. *Before reaching the "Cathedral", the route bends left and climbs steeply up a sharply bending path.* This, the most strenuous section of the walk, brings you up to the viewpoint at the ❺ **Mirador de la Ruleta**. Take in the vast, desolate Ucanca plain from which the giant rocks

300m 4 mins
❷ Roques de García
1,300m 20 mins
❸ Torre Blanca
1,300m 23 mins
❹ "Cathedral"
600m 23 mins
❺ Mirador de la Ruleta

rise like prehistoric stones with the rugged walls of Las Cañadas in the background.

TIME FOR SOME REFRESHMENT

500m 7 mins

❻ Parador Nacional

450m 6 mins

❶ Mirador de la Ruleta

Walk along the access road to the mirador until you reach the TF-21. Walk toward the pale purple building of the ❻ *Parador Nacional* ➤ p. 65. *Continue 450m further on until you reach* the cafeteria for a snack or the rustic restaurant for Canarian specialities while taking one long last look at Mount Teide before heading back (or taking the bus) to your starting point at the ❶ Mirador de la Ruleta.

INSIDER TIP
A break with a view

❺ A CYCLING TOUR OF THE SOUTHERN UPLANDS

➤ Explore the hills behind the southern beach resorts
➤ Visit eagles and exotic creatures
➤ Viewpoints, volcanic rocks and historic towns
➤ Even art connoisseurs will find something to admire
➤ Tenerife's longest beach
➤ Fancy a trip on a submarine?

📍 Los Cristianos

 Los Cristianos

🔄 63km

🚴 1 day (6 hrs total cycling time)

📶 Difficulty: medium (riders need to be in good physical condition)

ℹ️ Costs: mountain-bike rental from 18 euros (helmets are mandatory); admission **Jungle Park** 32 euros, and **Mariposa** 15 euros, with guided tour (reservation required: *mariposa@kulturpark-mariposa.de*) 25 euros; one-hour submarine trip from the ❿ **San Miguel Marina** 54.15 euros (book in advance: *submarinesafaris.com*).

DISCOVERY TOURS

Playa de Los Cristianos

ARONA AND A SCULPTURE PARK

Leave ❶ **Los Cristianos** ➤ p. 102 *on the TF-665 (signposted Chayofa/Arona). After the motorway roundabout, take the TF-28 and leave the town behind you*. The traffic ebbs away and the scenery becomes more rural. As you start to go uphill, you can look back at the resorts on the coast from a safe distance. Stop for a first coffee break in ❷ **Chayofa**, where ex-patriates live in flower-adorned bungalows. The cosy **Tasca del Arte de Chayofa** *(daily 3–11pm | Ctra General Antigua de Chayofa s/ | tel. 922 72 91 43 | €–€€)* offers tapas and has a garden terrace. Another attraction is the **Jungle Park** *(daily 10am–5.30pm | aguilasjunglepark.com),* which has tigers, sea lions, monkeys and a falconry show. From here, *continue along a road which joins the TF-51 which will take you up to the town of* ❸ **Arona** ➤ p. 115, at an altitude of 630m, with high mountains around it. It has an attractive plaza with a town hall, church and dense laurel trees in whose shade you can take a quick snooze. You then *head towards* ❹ **Túnez** *along a side road* where two gallery owners have created **Mariposa** *(C/ Túnez 63-A | kulturpark-mariposa.com),* a two-hectare art and sculpture park.

❶ Los Cristianos		
	4km	31 mins
❷ Chayofa		
	6.5km	1 hr 8 mins
❸ Arona		
	1km	3 mins
❹ Túnez		

One-hour submarine tours into the underwater world depart from the San Miguel Marina

5.5km	31 mins
❺ Mirador de la Centinela	
4.5km	23 mins
❻ San Miguel	
5.5km	37 mins
❼ Granadilla de Abona	
12.5km	42 mins

AMAZING VIEWS AND OLD-FASHIONED VILLAGES

In Valle de San Lorenzo, you return to the TF-28 and, after a few kilometres, you reach the ❺ Mirador de la Centinela, *which has the best views in the south. The road now begins to roll gently (but no steep hills!) to* ❻ San Miguel, *with its pretty church, cobbled streets and the ethnographic museum* Casa del Capitán *(closed Sat/Sun | C/ Calvario 1 | admission free). It's another 4km to* ❼ Granadilla de Abona, *a village that has grown hugely thanks to the tourism boom. However, its historic centre has retained its old charm. Next to the parish church and worth a visit is the former post office; today it is the restaurant* Senderos de Abona *(C/ Peatonal de la Iglesia 5 | senderosdeabona. es | €). Another restaurant,* Casa Tagoro ➤ p. 95, *is located in a historic mansion and offers memorable dishes created from the freshest of ingredients.*

THE BLISS OF THE DOWNHILL

Beyond Granadilla, you come to a well-earned downhill stretch: *zoom down the TF-64, continue 7.5km to the coast and over the TF-1 motorway until you reach*

DISCOVERY TOURS

❽ El Médano ➤ p. 93, 5km away. This, Tenerife's surfer paradise, has the longest natural beach on the island: it stretches for 3km at the foot of the Montaña Roja (Red Mountain). Take a dip in the waves! Playa de la Tejita ➤ p. 95, the beach just west of the Montaña Roja, is a popular nudist spot.

INSIDER TIP Pick your beach carefully

FRESH FISH AT THE HARBOUR

Now take the TF-643 along the coast to your next treat: the rows of restaurants and bars offering fresh seafood at the harbour in **Los Abrigos ➤ p. 95** – **❾ Perlas del Mar ➤ p. 95**, for example. After your meal, it's time to cycle along the coast via *Playa San Blas* and along the promenade to the **❿ San Miguel Marina**. If the timing is right, from the end of the pier you may be able to set off on a submarine excursion *(tel. 922 73 66 29 | submarinesafaris.com)* past schools of fish to a 30m-deep shipwreck. *Head back to* **❶ Los Cristianos ➤ p. 102** *on the flat TF-655;* it's an easy ride home!

❽ El Médano
7km 26 mins
❾ Perlas del Mar
3.5km 13 mins
❿ San Miguel Marina
12.5km 1 hr 5 mins
❶ Los Cristianos

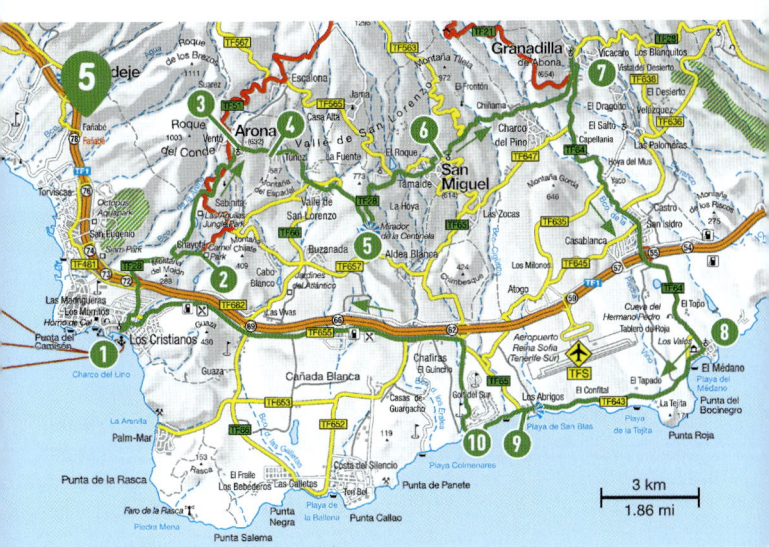

GOOD TO KNOW
HOLIDAY BASICS

ARRIVAL

AIR
Cheap flights are available from the UK and Ireland with Ryanair, easyJet and Thomas Cook (UK flight time about four hours). Book ahead and look out for deals to get the best prices – a return fare can cost anything between £50 and £350. There are two airports: the southern airport, *Reina Sofía* (aka *Tenerife Sur*), which is served by most international airlines, is a 20-minute drive from Playa de las Américas and Los Cristianos and about one hour from Puerto de la Cruz. Scheduled buses run from the southern airport to Los Cristianos and Costa Adeje (nos. 40, 343 and 711; approx. 4 euros), Santa Cruz de Tenerife (nos. 111 and 711; approx. 9.50 euros) and Puerto de la Cruz (no. 343; approx. 14 euros).

All Spanish internal flights and many low-cost airlines land at *Tenerife Norte* near La Laguna. Inter-Canary Island flights depart from here and also from *Reina Sofía* (information *aena.es*).

 No time difference

The Canary Islands operate on Western European Time (the same as GMT) from November to March and on Western European Summer Time (GMT +1) from April to October.

FERRY
Once a week a car ferry operated by Naviera Armas *(navieraarmas.com)* leaves from the southern Spanish port of Cádiz. The crossing to Santa Cruz de Tenerife takes approx. 40 hours. A fare for a single journey starts from 100

Teide National Park

euros per person (cabins and cars are extra). A car costs roughly the same as a passenger fare. Book through travel agencies, *directferries.co.uk* or *trasmediterranea.es*.

GETTING IN

All arrivals from the UK will be required to show a passport on arrival which must have at least six months' validity and must have been issued during the 10 years immediately before the date of entry. Check any other requirements with your airline before you fly.

CLIMATE & WHEN TO GO

Tenerife's mild climate means only small fluctuations in temperature. In the arid south, even in winter, temperatures hardly ever fall below 18°C and only rarely rise above 24°C. In summer the temperature can stay at 30°C and above for weeks. Even at moderate altitudes weak air currents can give rise to oppressive heat. The temperatures in the north are often significantly lower than in the south. In winter it can get cold at altitudes above 500m. Remember to pack a rain jacket and sweater along with your hat and sun cream. As water temperatures in Tenerife are always in the

OFFSET YOUR FLIGHT

The return flight is likely to be the most environmentally damaging part of your holiday. A single traveller on a return flight from London to Tenerife generates 998kg of CO_2. You can offset this emission at *myclimate.org* (and other organisations) for around £21. The money is used to fund climate protection projects around the world.

18–24°C range, it's fine to swim in the sea 365 days a year. The best time to visit the island is from November to March.

GETTING AROUND

BUS
Buses on Tenerife are called *guaguas* (pronounced guahuah). Green TITSA buses *(titsa.com)* run from Santa Cruz's central bus station, *Estación de Guaguas (Av. 3 de Mayo 47)*, to almost every town on Tenerife. You can buy a multi-fare "Ten+" ticket at bus stations in Santa Cruz and other holiday resorts. This gives holders a 30 per cent (or more) reduction on all fares (it does not apply on the 🍃 nos. 342/348 which go to Teide). There is also a one-day travel card for 10 euros and a seven-day travel card for 50 euros (available for download via the mobile app). Tram no. 1 runs every 5–15 minutes between Santa Cruz and the university town of La Laguna *(metrotenerife.com)*.

CAR HIRE
Car rental companies run offices in the airports, in all the holiday resorts and also in many hotels. Hire charges for a small car could well be less than 50 euros per day (including taxes and comprehensive insurance) for a week's hire. *Cicar (tel. 928 82 29 00 | cicar.com)* is a reliable local company, which has offices in every port and airport and most holiday resorts. The cars are well maintained, and the service is excellent if you break down. You must be over 21 to rent a car and firms will require a deposit.

RULES OF THE ROAD
The roads on Tenerife are good and safe. Maximum speed: in built up areas 50kmh; on country roads 90kmh; on motorways 120kmh; on single-lane roads 30kmh; and on roads with no defined pavements 20kmh. The breath-alcohol limit is 0.025%, which roughly corresponds to a blood-alcohol limit of 0.05% (stricter than the UK). Drivers must also keep a yellow vest in the car. Telephone calls may only be made using hands-free mobile phones.

Parking is not allowed where there are yellow markings by the kerb; a parking fee is payable where there are blue lines. Only licensed *grúas* are permitted to tow away vehicles.

TAXI
All taxis are licensed and fitted with meters, which must be turned on when you get into the car. On top of the basic fare, you pay supplements on Sundays and national holidays, at night and for port/airport trips as well as for bulky luggage. If you want to take a taxi for a day's tour, get a quote first.

TRAVELLING BETWEEN THE ISLANDS
You can get to all the other Canary Islands from Tenerife; timetables and prices can be found online from ferry

GOOD TO KNOW

operators *Fred Olsen (fredolsen.es)* and *Naviera Armas (navieraarmas.com)*, and ticket reservations are also possible via *directferries.co.uk*.

The one-way crossing (seat only) costs approx. 170 euros per person; a cabin, car transport and meals are charged extra. Prices are roughly the same as the domestic flights of the regional airlines *Binter (binternet.com)* and *Canary Fly (canaryfly.es)*.

EMERGENCIES

EMBASSIES & CONSULATES
UK CONSULATE
Mon–Fri 8.30am–1.30pm | Plaza Weyler 8, 1°, 38003 Santa Cruz de Tenerife | tel. 928 26 25 08

US CONSULATE
Edificio ARCA, C/ Los Martínez Escobar 3, Oficina 7, 35007 Las Palmas | tel. 928 27 12 59

EMERGENCY SERVICES
Dial 112 in an emergency for access to ambulance, fire, police and emergency medical service.

HEALTH
Holidaymakers with a European/Global Health Insurance Card (EHIC/GHIC) will be treated free of charge in health centres and hospitals associated with the Spanish Seguridad Social, the state social security system. Even so, you should always have adequate travel insurance. Make sure you receive a detailed receipt *(factura)* for any treatment received in order to claim reimbursement when you return home.

Pharmacies *(farmacias)* all display a green Maltese Cross. Use adequate protection against the intense sun: wear a hat and apply a high-factor sun cream. Tap water on Tenerife is not drinkable but you can buy mineral water in big bottles in supermarkets.

There are A&E departments in Santa Cruz and Playa de las Américas.

Santa Cruz de Tenerife: *Hospital Universitario Nuestra Señora de la Candelaria (Ctra Rosario 145 | tel. 922 60 20 00); Hospiten Rambla (La Rambla 115 | tel. 922 29 16 00 | hospiten.es).*

Playa de las Américas/Los Cristianos: *Espacio de Salud DKV (Mon–Fri 8am–8pm | Av. Antonio Domínguez (C.C. Zentral Center), Playa de las Américas | tel. 922 10 22 02); Hospiten Sur (24hr service and hotel visits | C/ Siete Islas 8 | tel. 922 75 00 22 | hospiten.es).*

Most doctors speak English but if you need complicated advice check online first.

ESSENTIALS

BANKS
You can withdraw money at ATMs using your debit card. However, the fees are often exorbitant, so check in advance with your bank and find out where you will get the best rates and deals. Bank opening times vary, but most are open Monday–Friday

8.30am–2pm and Saturday 8.30am–1pm. Credit cards are accepted virtually everywhere.

BEACHES

The longest (3km) natural beach on the island is at El Médano in the southeast. The beaches between Los Cristianos and Costa Adeje in the south are artificial but very attractive. One of the most picturesque beaches (also artificial) is Playa de las Teresitas, north of Santa Cruz. The north is famous for its black beaches of which Playa Jardín in Puerto de la Cruz is the nicest. Nudism is only allowed on a few beaches – Playa de la Tejita, west of El Médano, Playa de Montaña Amarilla (Costa del Silencio) and Playa de las Gaviotas, north of San Andrés.

CAMPING

Wild camping is prohibited. The island has several campsites, e.g. *Camping-Caravaning Nauta (Cañada Blanca, Ctra 6225, Km1.5, Las Galletas, Arona | tel. 922 78 51 18 | campingnauta.es); Tenerife Climbing House (La Asomadita 8, Arico | tel. 689 88 68 09 | tenerifeclimbinghouse.com) and the glamping Gaia La Segunda (Lomo de la Burra, Guía de Isora | tel. 634 17 02 32 | gaialasegunda.com)*.

CUSTOMS

There are strict customs rules when flying home from the Canary Islands (even within the EU). Check these carefully, but you are normally limited to 200 cigarettes, 1 litre of spirits and 2 litres of wine.

Adapter Type C

220 Volt alternating current. You will need a European adapter.

FESTIVALS & PUBLIC HOLIDAYS

1 Jan	Año Nuevo (New Year's Day)
6 Jan	Los Reyes (Epiphany)
Jan/Feb	Canary Islands International Music Festival)
March/April	Viernes Santo (Good Friday)
1 May	Día del Trabajo (Labour Day)
30 May	Día de las Islas Canarias (Canary Islands' Day)
May/June	Corpus Christi
25 July	Santiago Apóstol (St James' Day)
15 Aug	Asunción (Assumption)
12 Oct	Columbus Day
1 Nov	Todos los Santos (All Saints' Day)
6 Dec	Constitution Day
8 Dec	Immaculate Conception
25 Dec	Christmas

HOW MUCH DOES IT COST?

Coffee	from 1.50 euros for a cup of coffee
Petrol	about 2.40 euros for 1 litre of unleaded
Tapas	from 4 euros for a tapa
Taxis	3.50 euros basic fare plus 1 euro/km
Wine	from 2.50 euros for a small glass
Sun lounger	9–12 euros for a day

GOOD TO KNOW

LANGUAGE
In the larger resorts you will easily get by using English. However, a smattering of Spanish will come in very handy in more remote places or on public transport. See p. 147 for useful words and phrases.

OPENING HOURS
Shops are usually open from 9/10am until 8pm. Many smaller shops will take a siesta (1.30–5pm). On Saturday most smaller places are only open until 2pm. Big supermarkets and shopping centres stay open 9am–9pm. Most restaurants serve food 1–4pm and 7–11pm and in holiday resorts from noon until well into the night.

PHONE & INTERNET
Spain's international code is 0034, after which you type in the nine-digit number (starting with the local dialling code 922). To call home, the UK code is 0044, the US is 001 and Ireland is 01462 (then omit the first 0 of the number). Thanks to fibre optics, the internet works well on the island.

POST
You can buy stamps *(sellos)* at post offices *(correos)* and in newsagents *(estancos)*. Sending a letter *(carta)* or postcard *(tarjeta postal)* should cost between 1.50 euros and 2 euros. There are private postal services alongside the relatively reliable national company – these may be cheaper but are not always reliable.

PRICES
The price you will have to pay for food and services (e.g. car repairs) is likely to be about the same as in the UK or in the US. Leisure and theme parks are especially expensive (over 100 euros for a family of four). Cigarettes, cosmetics and some over-the-counter medicines are slightly cheaper than at home.

RURAL RETREATS
If you go on holiday to Tenerife, you don't have to stick to the coast. There are a number of agencies that rent out accommodation outside the major resorts, ranging from *fincas* that can sleep 10 people to a cave. They are normally pretty luxurious and prices are generally much lower than in hotels. *Casas Rurales* (country houses) are usually lovingly renovated and in beautiful locations.

TIPPING
If you are happy with service in a restaurant, round up the bill by about 10 per cent. Hotel staff expect tips, as do tour guides and taxi/coach drivers – again approx. 10 per cent of the bill is recommended.

TOURIST INFORMATION
Tourist information is available at spain.info and from the following tourist offices:

LONDON
6th Floor, 64 North Row | London W1K 7DE | info.londres@tourspain.es

DUBLIN
Callaghan House, 13-16 Dame St, Dublin D02 HX67 | dublin@tourspain.es

EDINBURGH
63 North Castle Street, Edinburgh EH2 3LJ | edinburghs@tourspain.es

NEW YORK
60 East 42nd St, Suite 5300 (53rd Floor) | New York, NY 10165-0039 | nuevayork@tourspain.es

TENERIFE
Arrivals hall of Reina Sofía Airport *(Mon-Fri 9am-9pm | Sat 9am-5pm | tel. 922 39 20 37)* and in all larger resorts on the island.

WEATHER IN TENERIFE

■ High season
■ Low season

	JAN	FEB	MARCH	APRIL	MAY	JUNE	JULY	AUG	SEPT	OCT	NOV	DEC
Daytime temperatures	21°	21°	22°	23°	24°	26°	28°	29°	28°	26°	23°	22°
Night-time temperatures	14°	14°	15°	16°	17°	19°	21°	21°	21°	19°	17°	16°
Hours of sunshine per day	5	6	7	8	10	11	11	11	9	7	5	5
Rainfall days per month	7	5	3	2	1	0	0	0	1	4	6	7
Water temperature in °C	19	18	18	18	19	20	21	22	23	23	21	20

WORDS & PHRASES

SMALLTALK

yes/no/maybe	sí/no/quizás
please/thank you	por favor/gracias
Hello/Goodbye/Bye	Hola/Adiós/Hasta luego
Good day/evening/night	Buenos días/Buenas tardes/Buenas noches
Excuse me/sorry! (informal/formal)	¡Perdona!/¡Perdone!
May I?	¿Puedo …?
Sorry?/Could you repeat?	¿Cómo dice?
My name is …	Me llamo …
What is your name? (formal/informal)	¿Cómo se llama usted?/¿Cómo te llamas?
I am from … the UK/USA/Ireland	Soy de … el Reino Unido/los Estados Unidos/Irlanda
I (don't) like this	Esto (no) me gusta
I would like … /Do you have …?	Querría …/¿Tiene usted …?
How much is …?	¿Cuánto cuesta …?
open/closed/opening hours	abierto/cerrado/horario
straight on/on the left/on the right	todo recto/a la izquierda/a la derecha
more/less	más/menos
Help!/Look out!/Be careful!	¡Socorro!/¡Atención!/¡Cuidado!
0/1/2/3/4/5/6/7/8/9/10/100/1000	cero/un, uno, una/dos/tres/cuatro cinco/seis/siete/ocho/nueve/diez/cien, ciento/mil

EATING & DRINKING

The menu, please	El menú, por favor
expensive/cheap/price	caro/barato/precio
Could you bring … please?	¿Podría traerme … por favor?
bottle/jug/glass	botella/jarra/vaso
knife/fork/spoon	cuchillo/tenedor/cuchara
salt/pepper/sugar	sal/pimienta/azúcar
vinegar/oil/milk/lemon	vinagre/aceite/leche/limón
cold/too salty/undercooked	frío/demasiado salado/sin hacer
with/without ice/fizz (in water)	con/sin hielo/gas
vegetarian/allergy	vegetariano/vegetariana/alergia
I would like to pay, please	Querría pagar, por favor
bill/receipt/tip	cuenta/recibo/propina

HOLIDAY VIBES
FOR RELAXATION & CHILLING

FOR BOOKWORMS & FILM BUFFS

🎥 ÓSCAR. THE COLOUR OF DESTINY (2008)
International co-production by Lucas Fernández about the life of the Canarian painter Óscar Domínguez, a contemporary and friend of Pablo Picasso. Many of his paintings are in the TEA in Santa Cruz.

🎥 CLASH OF THE TITANS (2009)
Who would have guessed that much of this Hollywood blockbuster starring Liam Neeson and Ralph Fiennes was filmed in Teide National Park.

🎥 JASON BOURNE (2016)
Paul Greengrass shot many scenes of the fifth installment of his *Bourne* film series (starring Matt Damon) in Tenerife. The island was chosen to illustrate places in Beirut, Athens and Reykjavík. The Plaza de España in Santa Cruz de Tenerife represented Syntagma Square in Athens.

📖 MORE KETCHUP THAN SALSA: CONFESSIONS OF A TENERIFE BARMAN (2005)
Joe Cawley's 2005 light-hearted look at life on the island from the viewpoint of a British expat.

PLAYLIST

0:58

LOS SABANDEÑOS – CANTATA DEL MENCEY LOCO
A traditional folk band singing mournfully about the "crazy Guanche rulers"

▶ **IDA SUSAL – SERÁ, SERÁ**
She takes inspiration from many sources – reggae, reggaeton and cumbia – and her lyrics often call out macho culture

▶ **SARA SOCAS – PIELES**
The *Tinerfeña* rapper became a star in the Spanish-speaking world thanks to her feminist lyrics

▶ **ARISTIDES MORENO – EL CAMBUYÓN**
Caustic social commentary from an old Canarian crooner

▶ **PEDRO GUERRA – CONTAMÍNAME**
Poetic singer-songwriter

The holiday soundtrack is available at **Spotify** under **MARCO POLO** Canaries

Or scan the code with the Spotify app

ONLINE

ARBOLAPP CANARIAS
Need help spotting dragos? This free app developed by various Spanish ministries allows you to identify trees on Tenerife.

ELCORAZONDETENERIFE.COM
"The heart of Tenerife" website comes with a free app and provides plenty of info on the capital and the Anaga Mountains.

RUTASTENERIFERURAL.COM
16 hiking routes (mainly in the north of Tenerife) with videos and maps.

I LOVE ARONA 2.0
This app is a great way to get to know the south of the island, with details of fun whale-watching trips.

STAR WALK
Enjoy the starry nights of Tenerife. The app can work out which way you are looking and tell you which stars you can see.

TITSA
With the Tenerife Bus Company app, you'll know where the next bus stop is and when the bus will arrive.

INDEX

Adeje 114
Aguamansa 54, 124
Águilas Jungle Park 115, 137
Alcalá 33
Aqualand 110
Arafo 93
Arguayo 30, 31, 61, 131
Arico 93
Arona 115, 125, 137
Artenerife 8, 31, 44, 74, 103, 109
ARTlandya 55
Auditorio de Tenerife 16, 71
Bahía del Duque 107, 125
Bailadero 129
Bajamar 9, 83
Barranco del Infierno 35
Basílica de Candelaria 90
Benijo 129
Boca de Tauce 125
Buenavista del Norte 59, 132
Camello Center 10, 59
Candelaria 86, 90
Casa de la Real Aduana 44
Casa del Carnaval 21, 71, 72
Casa Museo del Pescador 9, 44
Casas de Afur 129
Casas de los Balcones 51
Castillo de San Cristóbal 9, 73
Castillo de San Miguel 57
Castillo de San Felipe 44, 46
Centro Cultural El Tanque 71
Centro de Visitantes El Portillo 64
Centro de Visitantes Telesforo Bravo del Parque 51
Chayofa 137
Chinamada 84
Chío 119, 126
Convento de San Francisco 57
Costa Adeje 32, 107, 119, 140, 144
Costa del Silencio 106, 144
Cueva del Viento 56
Cumbre Dorsal 34, 66, 80
Drago Milenario 54, 134
El Caletón natural swimming pools 58
El Corte Inglés 30
El Cristo de los Dolores 81
El Médano 33, 34, 35, 86, 93, 97, 138, 139, 144
El Portillo 9, 47, 64, 80, 125
El Puertito de Güímar 93
El Sauzal 28, 81
El Tanque 59
farmers' markets 30
Forestal Park Tenerife 10, 32
Fundación Cristino de Vera 9
Garachico 56, 65, 133
Granadilla 95
Granadilla de Abona 138
Gran Canaria 76
Guía de Isora 118
Güímar 91
Hijuela del Botánico 52
Icod de los Vinos 11, 28, 58, 54, 133
Iglesia de Nuestra Señora de la Concepción, La Laguna 78
Iglesia de Nuestra Señora de la Concepción, Santa Cruz de Tenerife 71
Iglesia de Nuestra Señora de la Peña de Francia 44
Iglesia de San Francisco, Santa Cruz 72
Iglesia de Santa Ana, Garachico 58
Iglesia de San Marcos, Icod de los Vinos 55
Iglesia San Pedro Apóstol, Güímar 91
ITER 96
Jardín Botánico 44
Jardines del Marquesado de la Quinta Roja 52
La Caldera 124
La Caleta 32, 113
La Catedral de los Remedios 78
Lago Martiánez 10, 45
La Gomera 106
La Laguna 15, 16, 21, 66, 77–80, 85, 127, 128, 140, 142
La Matanza de Acentejo 82
La Orotava 21, 31, 50, 124
La Rambla, Santa Cruz 72
Las Cañadas 62, 65
La Victoria de Acentejo 82
Loro Parque 10, 45
Los Abrigos 95, 139
Los Cristianos 87, 102–106, 119, 137, 139, 140, 144
Los Gigantes 116, 131, 134
Los Realejos 49
Los Silos 8, 59
Macizo de Teno 60, 131
Masca 21, 61, 132
Mirador Cruz del Carmen 128
Mirador de Chío 127
Mirador de Chirche 126
Mirador de Jardina 128
Mirador de la Centinela 138
Mirador de la Ruleta 134, 135, 136
Mirador de Ortuño 80
Mirador Pico del Inglés 128
Montañas de Anaga 34, 66, 84
Museo Arqueológico Municipal 19, 44, 44
Museo de Artesanía Iberoamericana 52
Museo de Bellas Artes 72
Museo de Historia de Tenerife 78
Museo de la Ciencia y el Cosmos 78
Museo de la Naturaleza y el Hombre 19
Museo de la Naturaleza y el Hombre 72
Museo Muñecas 55
Observatorio del Teide 11, 65, 127
Paisaje Lunar, Vilaflor 97
Palmetum 72
Parque García Sanabria 72
Parque Marítimo César Manrique 75
Parque Nacional del Teide 8, 21, 22, 35, 62, 125
Parque Taoro 46
Parroquia de la Inmaculada Concepción de la Virgen María 51, 52
Paseo Marítimo 107
Pico del Teide 14, 17, 64, 125
Pico Viejo 64, 127
Pirámides de Güímar 11, 19, 91
Playa de Alcalá 117
Playa de Benijo 34
Playa de Fañabé 112
Playa de la Arena 117
Playa de las Américas 11, 33, 35, 107, 140, 143
Playa de las Gaviotas 105
Playa de las Teresitas 76, 130, 144
Playa de las Vistas 105
Playa de la Tejita 95, 139, 144
Playa del Camisón 112
Playa del Duque 112
Playa de Los Cristianos 105
Playa de los Guíos 117
Playa del Socorro 34
Playa de Martiánez 34, 43, 48
Playa de Montaña Amarilla 144
Playa El Bollullo 48
Playa El Médano 94
Playa Jardín 48, 127, 144
Playa Paraíso 116
Playa Punta Brava 34
Plaza de España, Santa Cruz 72
Plaza de la Candelaria, Santa Cruz 72
Plaza de la Constitución, La Orotava 52
Plaza de la Patrona de Canarias, Candelaria 90
Plaza del Ayuntamiento, La Orotava 53
Plaza del Charco, Puerto de la Cruz 43, 46, 48
Porís de Abona 93
Puerto de la Cruz 28, 33, 39, 42–48, 65, 124, 127, 140
Puerto Pesquero 46
Punta del Hidalgo 83
Punta de Teno 133
Roques de García 63, 125, 135
Ruta de los Molinos de Agua 53
San Andrés 16, 76, 130, 144
San Juan 118, 126
San Juan de la Rambla 50
San Marcos 56
San Miguel 138
San Miguel Marina 139
Santa Cruz de Tenerife 16, 17, 30, 66, 70–76, 87, 130, 140, 142, 143
Santiago del Teide 61, 131
Siam Park 10, 110
Tacoronte 28, 30, 81
Taganana 77
Tenerife Espacio de las Artes (TEA) 9, 16, 74
Tenerife Norte airport 140
Tenerife Sur airport (Reina Sofía) 15, 93, 140
Teno Massif 34, 39, 131
TF-38 119
Torre Blanca 135
Túnez 137
Valle de Guerra 82
Valle de La Orotava 15, 34, 38, 50, 124
Vilaflor 11, 97, 125
Virgen de Candelaria 22

INDEX & CREDITS

WE WANT TO HEAR FROM YOU!

Did you have a great holiday? Is there something on your mind? Whatever it is, let us know! Whether you want to praise the guide, alert us to errors or give us a personal tip – MARCO POLO would be pleased to hear from you. Please contact us by email:

sales@heartwoodpublishing.co.uk

We do everything we can to provide the very latest information for your trip. Nevertheless, despite all of our authors' thorough research, errors can creep in. MARCO POLO does not accept any liability for this.

PICTURE CREDITS
Cover picture: Playa de las Teresitas (Shutterstock: leoks)
Photos: DuMont Bildarchiv: M. Sasse (83); R. Freyer (84/85); I. Gawin (9, 151); R. Hackenberg (81); huber-images: A. Armellin (94/95), C. Dörr (20), O. Fantuz (113, 133, 148/149), Mirau (62/63), A. Piai (30/31, 140/141), R. Schmid (6/7, 24/25, 26/27, 38/39, 46, 49, 50/51, 55, 57, 60, 75, 92, 106, 109, 111, 127, 137), F. Vallenari (66/67), R. Wittek (120/121), J. Wlodarczyk (2/3, 98/99); Laif: M. Gumm (28, 73, 116), M. Sasse (96, 115), Tophoven (58); look-photos: H. Erber (32/33), B. Merz (12/13, 86/87, 91); lookphotos/age fotostock (35); mauritius images/age fotostock (79); mauritius images/AGF (back cover flap); mauritius images/Alamy: (11, 14/15, 45, 53, 105, 130), D. Herraez (8), A. Polo (27), Ch. Stirling (138); mauritius images/CuboImages (76/77); mauritius images/imagebroker (front cover flap/1, 10, 118/119); picture-alliance: R. Dirscherl (22); picture-alliance/Zoonar (103); Shutterstock: E. Wrba (18); D. Iacob (31); Melinda Nagy (34); vario images/Chromorange: W. G. Allgoewer (64); Salvador Aznar (146)

All rights reserved. No part of this book may be reproduced, stored in a retrieval system or transmitted in any form or by any means (electronic, mechanical, photocopying, recording or otherwise) without prior written permission from the publisher.

GPSR Compliance: MairDumont GmbH, Marco-Polo-Str, 73760 Ostfildern, Deutschland. Reference Tenerife5e/2505. Email: info@marcopolo.de

5th Edition – fully revised and updated 2025
Worldwide Distribution: Heartwood Publishing Ltd, Bath, United Kingdom
www.heartwoodpublishing.co.uk

© MAIRDUMONT GmbH & Co. KG, Ostfilder
Authors: Izabella Gawin, Sven Weniger
Editor: Christin Ullmann
Picture editor: Anja Schlatterer

Cartography: © KOMPASS-Karten GmbH, A-6020 Innsbruck/MAIRDUMONT, D-73760 Ostfildern (pp. 36–37, 122–123, 126, 129, 132, 139, back cover, fold-out map); Kompass Karten GmbH, A-Innsbruck © MAIRDUMONT, Ostfildern (p. 132); © MAIRDUMONT, Ostfildern, using mapping data under licence from OpenStreetMap, Licence CC-BY-SA 2.0 (pp. 36–37, 42–43, 68–69, 70, 88–89, 100–101, 104, 108).

Cover design and pull-out map cover design:
bilekjaeger_Kreativagentur with Zukunftswerkstatt, Stuttgart

Page design: Langenstein Communication GmbH, Ludwigsburg

Heartwood Publishing credits:
Translated from the German by Sophie Blacksell Jones, John Owen, Kathleen Becker, Jennifer Walcoff Neuheiser, Suzanne Kirkbright
Editors: Felicity Laughton, Kate Michell, Sophie Blacksell Jones
Prepress: Summerlane Books, Bath
Printed in India

MARCO POLO AUTHOR
IZABELLA GAWIN

Izabella only planned to spend one winter on the Canary Islands, but she felt so at home in the southern sun that she's been coming back every year – good-bye drizzle, farewell winter gloom! And because she found working on the Canaries as easy as living there, she ended up doing her PhD thesis on the islands and writing travel guides. Check out her blog *trip-to-go.com*!

DOS & DON'TS

HOW TO AVOID SLIP-UPS & BLUNDERS

DON'T SWIM IF THERE'S A RED FLAG
Many people underestimate the strength of the current and overestimate their own swimming ability. If a red flag is flying at the beach, you must stay out of the water. Yellow means "be careful", and if the flag is green, you can jump right in.

DON'T CAUSE A BLOCKAGE
Lots of Canarian privies politely plead that paper should not be flushed down the loo. The pipes in older buildings here are very narrow and block easily so, if you're asked to, please put your paper in the bin!

DO BUY SEEDS
Calla lilies and mini dragon trees – some visitors can't help but dig up these indigenous plants to give them a new home in their gardens. However, Canarian plants are subject to special protection and they must not be removed from the islands. Instead, buy a packet of seeds in a flower shop (*jardinería*) – but first check your country's import rules.

DO ASK BEFORE YOU EAT
Bread is part of every meal in Spain and once upon a time it was always free. Today it is often placed on your table … before appearing on your bill. It is a good idea to ask if it is *por cuenta de la casa* ("on the house").

DON'T WEAR FLIP-FLOPS IN THE MOUNTAINS
Tourists often start their trips in summery clothes on the coast only to be surprised by icy temperatures later on. The rule of thumb is: for every 100m in elevation, the temperature drops by 1°C. So, take a warm coat and suitable footwear.